NARCISSISTIC MOTHERS AND GROWN DAUGHTERS

THE HELL OF NARCISSISTIC FAMILY. HEALING GUIDE ON HOW TO HANDLE MANIPULATIVE PARENTS AND OTHER ABUSES, FIX THE RELATIONSHIP AND HEAL EMPATHY

CECILIA OVERT

Copyright © 2019 Cecilia Overt
All rights reserved.

No part of this book may be reproduced in any form or by any electronic or mechanical means, including photocopying, recording, or by any information storage and retrieval system now known or hereafter invented, without written permission from the publisher. The only exception is by a reviewer, who may quote short excerpts in a published review.

This document is aimed to provide accurate and reliable information in the light of the selected topic and all covered issues. This book is sold with the idea that the publisher is not required to render an officially permitted, accounting, or otherwise, qualified services. If advice is required in any way, professional or legal, seasoned experts of the profession should be consulted.

Every information given herein is claimed to be consistent and truthful, in case of any liability, with regard to inattention or otherwise, by any use or abuse of processes, policies, or directions contained within is solely the responsibility of the recipient reader. Under no conditions will any blame or legal responsibility be held against the publisher for any damages, monetary loss or reparation, due to the information herein.

The information herein is provided entirely for informational purposes, and it is universal. The information is provided without any type of guarantee assurance or a contract.

The trademarks that are used within the document are without any consent, and the publication of the trademark is without the backing of the trademark owner or any support. All brands and trademarks used within this book are to clarify the text only, and they are owned by their owners, not affiliated with this publication. Respective authors of the publication own all copyrights not held by the publisher.

Table of Contents

Introduction

Chapter 1 - The Narcissistic Mother

Chapter 2 - Behaviors of a Narcissistic Mother

Chapter 3 - Types of Narcissistic Mothers

Chapter 4 - Daughters and Mothers

Chapter 5 - Effects of Being Raised by a Narcissistic Parent

Chapter 6 - Mental Manipulation and Control

Chapter 7 - Abuse by a Narcissistic Mother

Chapter 8 - Separation and Healing

Chapter 9 - Overcoming Enmeshment

Conclusion

Introduction

One of the best tools I have used to heal myself and my traumas due to my relationship with my narcissistic mother is education. Educating yourself on everything that you can around narcissistic personality disorder, how it plays out in mother-daughter relationships, and how it has directly affected you as well as your symptoms can support you understand what you are experiencing. With this increased understanding, you can begin to identify where you are experiencing symptoms of this dysfunctional relationship in your life, why, and what can be done to help you heal them.

Let's start at the beginning of the equation: your mother. Your mother has likely been narcissistic since well before you were born, meaning you have been exposed to her narcissistic behaviors all your life. You have probably never known anything different. For this reason, we can conclude that the beginning of your problems around this starts with your mother and her disorder.

What Does Narcissistic Personality Disorder Look Like?

Narcissistic personality disorder itself is a mental condition that gives people an inflated sense of self-importance, dysfunctional relationships, an excessive deep-seated need for attention and admiration, and a complete lack of empathy for other people. Even though this is what they are experiencing, their symptoms can look somewhat different on the outside. This is because narcissists develop what are known as "masks" which are a sort of alter-ego that they hide behind to cover up the fact that there is something wrong with the way they behave. They use these masks to fake empathy, create false relationships with people in a way that does not reflect who they are truly are, and to create a genuine belief within themselves and others that there is nothing wrong with them.

The symptoms you are likely to see in a narcissist include an incredibly exaggerated sense of self-importance which often manifests as them behaving as if they are better than everyone else, and lying to make others believe it is true, too. They also have a sense of entitlement and feel as though they should get everything they want, including unlimited amounts of admiration for what they do. They often want to be recognized as superior to others, even without a reason to be recognized as so, and they fantasize about having unlimited success, power, brilliance, and beauty. A narcissist will also obsess over having the perfect everything in life, including the perfect house, the perfect mate, the perfect friends, and the perfect anything else. In their opinion, perfect things match their perfection, adding to their level of superiority over everyone else.

Narcissists can often be seen monopolizing conversations while also belittling or looking down on people who they believe to be inferior to themselves. They will often have a few people they seem to belittle the most, which are generally the ones who end up being their long-term victims for narcissistic abuse in many ways. However, they will belittle just about anyone as long as they can get away with it without tarnishing their perfect image, even though this image is all in their minds. Their inflated sense of self-importance also leads to them believing that they should get anything they want in life, no questions asked. They genuinely believe that people should just give in to what they desire without any struggles or difficulties in making it happen. Because of this, they will frequently take advantage of other people and treat them badly, with seemingly no understanding as to what they are doing and no compassion or empathy for the outcome of their actions.

Despite what it looks like on the outside, narcissists are highly envious of others which is largely the reason behind their constant bragging and self-inflating behaviors. They believe that when they act in these exaggerated ways that others envy them and wish to be them, which gives them an even larger feeling of self-importance.

The combination of all of their symptoms leads to narcissists being arrogant, haughty, conceited, pretentious and boastful. They are often the ones that appear confident to a fault, often to the point where people do not even believe that they are as confident as they truly claim to be. However, this is not always the case. Many narcissists have mastered experiencing an inflated sense of self-importance without coming across as overly confident, arrogant, or pretentious because they have come to realize that this does not serve their bigger mission. If they have come to realize that this behavior does not afford them the admiration and affection they desire, they will often tone down their behavior to increase the admiration and affection they receive. They can expertly shapeshift to fit any situation they need to, to get what they desire from that situation.

In private settings, narcissists are extremely unpredictable. They have severe interpersonal problems and can easily feel as though they have been wronged by others, leading to them reacting with rage. They may also react with rage or impatience if they feel that they are not receiving adequate special treatment from those around them. Narcissists struggle to deal with stress, regulate their emotions and behavior, and adapt to change. They can often become moody and depressed because they see their shortcomings and it makes them feel worse about themselves, which triggers their deep-seated insecurities, shame, and humiliation that they feel. These deep-seated feelings often come from realizing that they are not the same as others and fighting desperately to fit in, yet not knowing how to do so in a way that is not abusive and damaging to those around them. Even so, they will never admit this to anyone, under any circumstances.

What Causes Narcissistic Personality Disorder?

The true cause or causes of narcissistic personality disorder are not known. Doctors cannot pinpoint any one thing that causes narcissism in people, so there is no way of knowing what may have caused your mother's condition. With that being said, some psychologists and doctors have come to suspect that a series of three things can contribute to narcissistic personality disorder. These three things include the environment, genetics, and neurobiology. There is no guarantee that these are the reasons, but they are suspected to at least contribute to the development of narcissistic personality disorder.

The environment is believed to affect the development of narcissism when an individual is raised by a parent who either excessively adores or excessively criticizes the child. If your mother was raised by parents who were poorly attuned to your mother's needs and who overly babied her or who excessively criticized her, this may have contributed to her narcissism. She may have also directly inherited it from her parents. As well, there may be an alteration in your mothers' brain that creates a disconnect between behaviors and thoughts, which contributes to the development of narcissistic personality disorder.

Are There Any Cures for Narcissistic Personality Disorder?

Because there are no known causes for narcissism, there is no known cure for it, either. Furthermore, most people who have narcissistic personality disorder will not acknowledge that they have it and so they will never take action to attempt to treat their narcissism. As a result, they end up having it for life and there are unlikely to be any improvements in their symptoms. Despite what you may think, if a person with narcissism does not want to admit that they have this disorder, which they are highly unlikely to, there is nothing you can do to make them see the truth. They will never truly see, accept, or own their behaviors and actions because this is in direct contradiction to what they are attempting to achieve.

If a narcissist does agree to get treatment, the best thing they can do is attend therapy. Independent therapy and family therapy are both methods that can be used to help a person with narcissism understand how they are affecting those around them, and how their behaviors can be changed and improved. In some cases, changes may occur and the individual may become easier to be around.

Chapter 1 - The Narcissistic Mother

The way narcissism manifests in mothers specifically is unique, as children see their parents in a way that no one else does. Even a healthy relationship between a child and a parent is likely to be experienced in a way that is unique to them, not anyone else. Mothers tend to be more comfortable around their children, meaning that they can open up and express their true selves better around their children. For mothers who do not have narcissism, this is generally shown in a gentler and softer, nurturing manner. For those mothers who do have narcissism, however, this is generally a relationship where the narcissism will play out in a far more offensive and overwhelming manner than it would in any other relationship. In other words, narcissistic mothers tend to abuse their children, especially their daughters, more than anyone else. Understanding how narcissism manifests in mothers is the best way to identify where your mother is abnormal compared to other mothers, and how these abnormalities are linked to her narcissistic personality disorder.

A Mother That is Threatened by Her Child

Narcissistic mothers often experience the feeling of being threatened by their children in the sense that they worry that their children are likely to take attention and admiration away from themselves. When narcissistic mothers notice their children are getting attention around any given subject, such as excelling in school, they will often begin to feel threatened and will attempt to minimize the value of the child's achievements.

A big way they do this is through how they talk to others, using sayings like:

- "Finally, you're good at something for once!"
- "It's about time you bring home an award for something."
- "Wait, you mean you did something good? Wow."

Speaking in a way that makes it seem like the child is otherwise terrible is a way that a narcissistic mother can control the amount of attention the child receives. They may receive attention around this one thing, but through her words, she tarnishes the child's reputation and therefore prevents the child from receiving further accolades anywhere else in their lives. This way, she can earn those accolades for herself and gain all of the excessive attention and admiration she needs from others.

An Effort at Self-Fulfillment Through You

Another big way that narcissistic mothers can be identified through their symptoms is through attempting to inflate their sense of self through you. My mother often did this by attempting to take credit for every positive thing I did in my life, making it appear as though she was the only reason, I had anything good going for myself. She would frequently use this as a way to take the attention away from me and put it on herself, even when it did not make reasonable sense for her to do so.

For example, as a child, I used to get excellent grades in school and every time my report card came home with several A's on it my mom would make dinner complete with all of my favorite things, which happened to be her favorites, too. She would go on to say how this was going to be an evening to celebrate me and my achievements, making me feel like maybe

I had finally received her praise. Maybe she was finally proud of me. Every time, however, she would spend the entire dinner – my special dinner – talking about how she was responsible for my success. She would say things like how I would not be here without her, and how this proves that she is such a great mother, even going so far as to point out that I was cruel and mean for claiming otherwise when I called her out on her abuse to a family member one time

To add insult to injury, any time I would ask my mother for help with my homework she would either downright refuse or spend the entire time yelling at me for not being good enough, although it was her who was misunderstanding the assignments. In other words: I earned those A's in spite of her, not because of her. Over time I grew so resentful that I stopped caring about my grades at all because it was painful to have something, I was proud of ripped away and used as a tool against me constantly.

Narcissistic mothers frequently live through their children or use their children as a way to further inflate their sense of self. They generally do this because they know that at young ages children are not able to identify what is going on, and therefore they cannot stop the abuse from happening. By the time they are old enough to speak up, the mother has either made them too afraid to try or has already groomed everyone else to believe that the child is a problematic liar so that no one believes the child. In the end, the child is forced to live in a mental prison that is shaped and manned by their parent, which is a form of torture that no child should ever have to experience.

The Development of a Superficial Image

Another way that you can spot a narcissistic mother is in how they portray themselves to people outside of your family, or even outside of your relationship with her. Yes, narcissistic mothers will frequently wear several different masks even within one household, for example: abusing her child in private and pretending nothing ever happened when the child's father is around.

The development of a superficial image that portrays your mother as someone who never does anything wrong is a strategy that she uses to protect herself from her consequences. She does this to groom others into believing her, and not her child, which means that she can protect her primary source of being able to fulfill her cruel and unusual needs. This way, when she openly belittles and bullies her child the people around her believe it is warranted and the child has no hopes of escaping the experience.

Chapter 2 - Behaviors of a Narcissistic Mother

The child with Narcissistic Personality Disorder enters into adulthood with this disorder, which makes forming relationships difficult and impedes satisfaction. They are constantly subjected to internal conflict and always depend psychologically on others. The child is not an object of love that is raised consciously and selflessly; far from it. The child of the narcissistic mother is a mirror by which to gaze at and admire or deplore her.

Narcissistic mothers tend to fall into two basic classifications: smothering mothers and negligent mothers, both of which are discussed in detail below.

Smothering Mothering

The smothering mother, also known as the engulfing mother, cannot determine the boundaries between mother and daughter. The daughter is an appendage of the mother's self in her mind. What is a natural inclination from birth through the toddler stage becomes a problem later when the child is seeking autonomy. It happens surreptitiously, perhaps unconsciously on the part of both actors—mom and daughter. However, the mother does not want to let go; she maneuvers to impede maturity. The proper boundaries are not established, and normal bonding is thus interfered with.

This type of mothering intrudes in the friendships and communications of the growing girl. The girl's private space may be invaded without notice. There are prying questions. The narcissistic engulfing mother also tends to project her own preferences on the daughter, claiming that she really likes this or that type of food or fashion or whatever, rather than the one that the daughter says she likes.

Another negative mothering behavior on the part of the narcissistic-smothered woman is meddling in the daughter's relationships. Typically, she puts down a close friend or husband or schemes to make them unhappy with a view to disrupting a good relationship. She does this out of envy and resentment.

From this behavior mentioned above, the daughter feels pressure not to assert herself and her own tastes and choices. She may not readily stand up to the mother because of the perceived associated risks of anger on the part of the mother or unfair criticisms and other demonstrations of rejection. Should the daughter demand to distance themselves, the mother will persist nonetheless. It could lead to actual stalking and other forms of harassment.

The engulfing type often idealizes her girl in the extreme. Sometimes the daughter is always the reason for the mom's problems and shortcomings. In other cases, she is just plain cold and negligent, absorbed as she is in her own self-admiration and selfishness. Her tactics vary, corresponding to each of these three styles.

To the engulfing mom, there is only the mother. There is no daughter, from her perspective, so the mother assigns herself the right to control and intrude. She may engage in asserting her right as a mother while treating the grown daughter as a little child. She may seek to disturb the balance between relationships by coming between a third person and the daughter (i.e., triangulation).

Others may be fooled. Since the narcissist can be charming and alluring, even charismatic but certainly talkative in the interest of monopolizing the attention in any social circumstances, they may show admiration for the mother-daughter rapport they observe. It can appear to be an ideal relationship, one that is very close rather than pathologically domineering.

From Clinginess to Absence

Next, we proceed to the other end of the spectrum, the mother who ignores the daughter. This kind of mother is so self-absorbed that she has little time or thought for her daughter. Naturally, the impact is quite painful and confusing.

The mother may be physically present most of the time but does not engage with the daughter. She remains withdrawn from the relationship with the daughter and preoccupied with herself and her own activities or ideas. Approaches may only achieve annoyance from this mother. She does not want to listen. She is negligent about the normal duties of parenting: from personal grooming and hygiene, counseling about life, to household organization.

Attempts to raise issues or inquire as to why the mother is so distant get few responses. The reply is more likely to be the cold shoulder or some pretext to move away and refrain from conversation. The reader can well imagine the lack of affection in these circumstances. Any hugging may only be mechanical and tentative on the part of the mother who likes to ignore the child. There are no questions about how the school is going or how the girl is feeling, etc. There are never any compliments. No encouragements. Any conversation likely is conducted with an arrogant or condescending tone.

As the child grows up and carries on her life, there are no phone calls or invitations. Any recognition of a birthday or some other special occasion such as a graduation is addressed nominally, superficially. If any gifts appear, they are according to the mother's own tastes and pushed forward as if the daughter may not be intelligent enough to see its value and suitability, even if the gift is not at all relevant or likable to the younger woman.

Unlike the clingy relationship of the smothering mother, the engulfing, it is easy to remove oneself from the company or attention of the ignoring mom. Regardless, the pain of the emotional and material neglect cuts deep. The daughter can feel unworthy in general as a result. She may not trust other people enough to build close relationships after the experience with this mother. She may feel she never belongs or is unlovable.

Precious Doll or Cause of All Trouble?

It is also important to be aware of the dual danger of the mothers who either imagine a Golden Girl who can do no wrong or the Problem Child who spoils everything. Should a narcissistic mother have two children, she may assign each one of these opposing roles in the family. Projecting her internal idealization of herself, she exaggerates the attributes and accomplishments of the child she sees as golden. She sits on a privileged and beautiful pedestal above others. This one can never do anything wrong, in her eyes. Any bad behavior or weakness is dismissed while any success or positive feature, no matter how small, is elevated. The narcissistic parent of this one will shower this family member with rewards and support, such as money for clothes, lessons, trips, etc.

Conversely, the scapegoat child is branded the black sheep. All problems of the family, especially those of the mother, are supposedly because of her. This one is placed low on the totem pole, in a dark corner to be spat upon and cursed. Any achievement or positive attribute is squelched or ignored. She is unattractive or even ugly, socially inept, academically stunted, physically repulsive, and so on and so on. She is not worth investing any support in at all.

Should there really be two children forced into taking up opposing functions like this, they no doubt fight and compete. The golden girl has a license to criticize the scapegoat, but the scapegoat child can never win a battle or argument in this household. It is the scapegoat who likely will be punished should friction between them get out of control.

The narcissist certainly does not want to accept that the child labeled the scapegoat is right about anything; nor does she wish to find fault about anything to do with the child given the golden role. Doing either would lead to the narcissist to discover her own weaknesses and mistakes. She does not want to recognize the achievements of the scapegoat child; in fact, that child may be rewarded for failure (e.g., receiving hugs or gifts as signs of love only when something goes wrong).

Indeed, she may be conceived of having something wrong with her, being sick in some way. On the other hand, no recognition of any fault or problem with the golden girl will be made. Her achievements are inflated and over-compensated. She is a healthy one doing well, always.

Therefore, the one that is seen as the problem child probably will develop some medical issue such as an eating disorder or depression. The neuroses of the opposite figure are different—perhaps blossoming into a narcissist herself but certainly having anxiety about living up to perfection. There could be other bad habits such as deceit and manipulation so as to help the narcissist mother keep up the façade. Perhaps, the scapegoat child is the one with the greatest advantage, in the end, however. That's because neglect can drive her to become independent while the smothered child may never be free of the mother's domination, idealization, and control. The latter will have less baggage than the former.

Fathers Who Enable the Narcissistic Mother

What about the narcissistic mother's partner who is the father figure for the daughter? How does he respond? What's his parenting style in the face of his narcissistic spouse?

Unfortunately, in most instances, chances are, he is an enabler. If not the enabler, he probably shares the disorder or has taken off. Should he wish to stick around, how? He would have to support the narcissism.

The father in this type of scenario may be dysfunctional if he too is narcissistic. If he is not, however narcissistic, it is likely that he worships his wife, no matter what, otherwise, the father who is physically present plays along with the defensive narcissistic mom. Out of fear, he adopts the position of the sidekick to echo and assist. He becomes passive and lets the narcissism play out, despite the harm to the daughter, himself, and the woman.

He may become the guy who does the dirty work of attacking the daughter so that the mother can always appear correct, the enforcer deployed to either keep the daughter subjugated to the mother or prevent rebellion. He may rationalize the mother's wrong words and actions. If his partner gets angry, he follows suit or defends her with even greater rage. He may accuse the daughter of being a problem, endeavoring to make her feel ashamed or guilty, should she protest her treatment and desire her freedom and respect.

In most instances, the relationship between the narcissistic mother and the father is one of co-dependency, not love. The father may be anxious about maintaining the structure imposed by the mother and fear change or instability, so he entrenches himself in the accepting attitude and sets himself up as the prop onto which his leading star can lean.

Bloodsucking

The narcissistic woman, with her inflated sense of self and hypersensitivity to problems and criticism, may thrive on drama. The ignoring narcissist tends to make a big deal of the events in their lives and the effects on their emotional state while paying no heed to or suppressing the daughter's ups and downs. This parent is not interested in the disappointments, joys and exciting episodes of her own daughter's life; rather she makes the most of her own.

Everything is supposed to revolve around her. She may even dramatize the experience of others—neighbors, other family members, co-workers or business associates—so as to counter-pose them to her child's experience and try to make her child's life seem smaller. The smothering mother may tell the daughter she is just being a baby when the daughter mentions some trouble or goes through a defeat or disappointment. She may use the daughter's experience to underline the necessity of the daughter remaining under the wing of the engulfing mother, turning it into a justification for not spreading her wings to venture outside of the relationship.

Narcissistic mothers are like a vampire because they prey on the suffering of other people around them. She might display pleasure at passing on bad news for her child. She may exaggerate the misfortunes of others and their consequences and attach causes such as a person (here the child's) inabilities, unluckiness or deficiencies. Think of it—a miscarriage, a break-up, a rejection from a study program—the mother blames the daughter for these saddening and unfortunate events. This parent would most certainly deny any responsibility were there any that lead to disappointment.

Even at a funeral, the narcissist wants to make herself the focus of attention. She interprets what is happening as being related to her. For example, she may imagine that she was specially invited to attend because of her importance, not out of a duty to pay respect and express condolences. She may go on about how drastically the death hit her, not the tragedy it may mean for the deceased person and their loved ones. Accusations that this woman is thriving on the tragedies of others would be stymied. They would hit a brick wall. Well, denial is a hallmark of many disorders, no?

Chapter 3 - Types of Narcissistic Mothers

If you've dealt with a narcissistic mom, chances are that one of two things happened: you were very controlled, or you were ignored.

Or you could have seen a combination of both of those, but in any case you were robbed of a healthy normal childhood and very often face more struggles as an adult.

The Severe Narcissistic Overt Mother

This kind of mother is going to make you feel unloved because she is so self-absorbed. She's completely self-absorbed and always seeking attention. Life for her is a stage where she always has to be the star. Such mothers can bring up their kids, show them off to their friends and tell them, "You see what I have produced; my kids are my pride and joy."

This can be very damaging for boys because then the boys are learning that this is the only way to be in the world. To always be the kind of a man she expects him to be, he can't be fully himself.

When her daughter becomes a young woman, the overt narcissistic mother begins to compete with her, which can turn really nasty very quickly. This kind of mother is going to show you also how much burden you are to her. Once again self-absorption takes the upper hand, and she will tell you how much money it caused her to raise you and how much you are draining her because she just never has time for herself.

One day the narcissistic mother will push you out of the nest. She will want you out as soon as possible. She will want you to grow up without giving you the proper tools to go out into the world and succeed.

Other overt narcissistic mothers are the opposite; they want to keep you with them always, and forbid you to leave them because they will feel so abandoned. So she will reward you with co-dependency.

Another kind of overt narcissistic mother wants to feel needed and yet at the same time she's going to push you away when your needs become too much. She does not want you to be too self-reliant or independent, because then there is the threat of you not meeting her needs.

The overt narcissistic mother will not acknowledge your emotions; there's no room for you to fully express yourself basically because the moment you take up too much space, you're threatening her.

So she will always try to tear you down, but she will not acknowledge when she hurts you. She will say things that should never be said.

After you reach that competitive level with her, when you begin to turn into an independent teenage girl who now has her own life, she will continue to tear you down so she can keep building herself up. This woman has to always be on top.

She will try to hang out with your friends, and she'll even try to take over your peer group. She is the kind of woman who always wants to be perpetually young. She will also triangulate between siblings.

Triangulation is incredibly toxic especially in a family. Narcissistic mothers will whisper one thing to one child, another thing to another child, set them against each other, create conflict, and sit back to enjoy the drama that they have just created.

If later in life you've been able to dig for the truth and figure out what really happened, you can confirm your stories with the stories of your brothers or sisters or cousins—the more the better—then you'll be able to hopefully see a much more accurate picture.

Unfortunately, the dynamics of the average family these days is often more or less divided and usually there's more dysfunction and less sanity, because being the outspoken person will cost you so much.

This may cost you banishment, which is encoded in our genes as the worst form of punishment. When you're outside of the clan, when you've been pushed away from the tribe, you're out and therefore can be threatened by all sorts of predators. This is why loneliness also can feel so devastating to us because we feel threatened and exposed.

You'll never feel heard or seen or be able to succeed, so you're going to be trapped between the shame and guilt. If you don't do enough you're going to be ashamed, if you do too much you're going to feel guilty. Either way she will make you feel awful.

I've heard of young daughters being very successful only to find that their success threatens their relationship with their mother. What happens is that the mother feels she is not able to enjoy the full harvest of her daughter's success because the daughter has made a choice between her success and her mother.

Now, if the daughter knew the person she was dealing with, it may be much easier to make the decision of not going back to the toxic mother. But because of the idea that mothers need to be revered and you dare not separate yourself from them, the daughter is in conflict.

The overt narcissistic mother will give really conflicting messages, like proudly showing you off on the one hand, then subtly cutting you down on the other.

The Severe Narcissistic Sadistic Mothers

These mothers lock up their kids in their rooms. They are often alcoholics and completely neglectful and deep level of abandonment. Sometimes there are a series of new husbands. These step- fathers sometimes sexually abuse these kids, creating an unhealthy environment to raise a child. So many families don't deserve to raise kids because they simply will not provide a safe environment.

Unfortunately, the result of that is a very high number of people raised this way learn to fend for themselves. They have been shattered inside because they haven't received the sustenance, love, compassion, and protection they needed as children by virtue of being born.

Adult children of this kind of narcissistic mother will surely have a Complex Post Traumatic Stress Disorder (CPTSD).

The Enmeshed Mother

She is the most covert narcissistic mother. Instead of teaching you to build a life of your own, she snaps on the emotional handcuffs and never lets you go.

Emotional mothers can seem like they're just perfect, always taking care of their kids, but instead are turning their children into life long infants. The enmeshed mother will never allow you to grow up. If you're a man you'll always be stuck between this half man-half child situation. Children in this situation are emotionally stunted in so many ways because they have been imprinted with the message that it's not safe outside of the home, and that it is always better to be here with mom.

This is a form of co-dependency training that doesn't allow the children to go out there and learn the skills of survival and assertiveness in order to succeed. Their independence is not being supported and instead they are being punished for trying to be self-sufficient.

This can be extremely damaging for men, especially boys, because there's a borderline component here and that is the fear of abandonment. The narcissistic mother wants to pour all of her love, all of her attention into the kids and make them the centre of her world and oftentimes this is a result of a bad relationship with the father of her children.

If the father isn't gone, most of the time he neglects the children. He neglects his wife especially, and she will turn him into a monster in the boy's eyes, and the boy is then going to take over the burden of the dad who is not present.

So the son is going to have to grow up very quickly and will be rewarded for being there for his mommy. He will essentially become her surrogate husband. It's something that's called parentification.

This sometimes creates really sensitive, openhearted and giving men, but the problem is that their boundaries are very permeable. There is not enough give-and-take in the relationship and they will just work themselves to the bone to satisfy a woman, because that's what they did for their mothers. They will take that outside of the relationship with their mom and continue this dynamic in their romantic relationships. The problem with this is that it's very easy for other narcissists, sociopaths, psychopaths, and borderline women to be attracted to this kind of man and then destroy him.

So, the enmeshing mother may think in her mind that she's doing the right thing but she's not; she is suffocating her children. A healthy relationship between a parent and a child, especially a mother and a child, has to come from respect and the giving of space.

Children need to feel like they can fully be themselves and develop to whatever seed they were, so they can become the person that they were meant to become. A good healthy parent will support that independence and that separation.

Chapter 4 - Daughters and Mothers

When you have a baby, it's an incredible experience. You find that you're officially a parent of life. While most women relish this moment, planning awesome things for their children, the daughter of a narcissistic mother dreads everything about having had this child. The anxiety she feels about her baby is beyond crippling.

What exactly is she worried about? She is concerned that she might end up treating her child exactly the way her mother treated her. This is understandable, as she had no good model of what a loving parent-child relationship should be like. She worries she will leave her children's emotional needs ignored. She fears she is not up to the task of being a good mother. It could be just a belief or a knowing that you do not have the knowhow.

Usually, before the pregnancy even happens, you're probably already apprehensive about being a mother. You are deathly afraid of getting pregnant. Kids are not on your agenda. You'd rather have a dog. "Just as a test run," you tell yourself, even though you know deep down you're only interested in having a fur baby, and not a human one.

You worry that you might become just as abusive as your mother was to you. You fear that you will not connect with your child, just like your mother never bothered to connect with you.

Not Your Run-of-the-Mill Anxiety

Yes, it's not unusual for most mothers-to-be to be worried about how best to be a parent to their children. However, for the daughter of a narcissistic mother, her concerns are far beyond the usual. She is concerned about breaking the abusive cycle of narcissism. This can be pretty tough to do when you've never had a role model. You basically have to play this by ear.

When you do realize that you're making errors in the process of being a parent, do not beat yourself up, and definitely do not allow panic to take over you. Despite the fact that you may have learned one or two parenting traits that are completely narcissistic from your mother, that does not mean you are incapable of changing, or that you're a narcissist, too. The fact that you're able to recognize where you've gone wrong with parenting is in itself a good thing because you can now take steps to correct it and do better by your child.

The Other Extreme

I must warn you to be very careful about simply deciding to do the exact opposite of everything your mother did. If you do this, you might wind up recreating the same dynamics which held sway in your relationship with your own mother.

When you're looking to create something different from what you've always known, it's all too common to fall into the trap of thinking in non-negotiable terms of black and white. If your mother was always prone to rage, anger, and lashing out at you, the temptation would be for you to become the exact opposite of what she was. Passive, not bothering to assert yourself even if it's clearly needed, quiet when you should speak up, meek even when you should not be. The fact is that choosing to react this way when you're angry does not change the underlying emotions you feel.

You need to find balance.
Essentially, you want to find the middle ground in all of this. The middle ground will contain stuff that you value, and stuff your mother believes. There is nothing wrong with this. For instance, you might like a clean home, just like your mother. There's nothing wrong with that. You may, however, choose to go about encouraging your children to keep the home clean in a much different manner than your mother did. One in which the children do not feel threatened, and are actually highly motivated to help keep things spic and span.

Just as your mother expected you to have good grades, you definitely expect the same of your children. Unlike your mother, however, you could be encouraging, supportive, willing to hear them out so you can understand what they're struggling with, and willing to work with them to help them get good grades without putting any undue pressure on them, or making them feel like you love them less because they're unable to attain a certain grade. The whole point of this is you do not need to do a complete one-eighty just because you're trying so hard not to be your mother.

If you had a blanking mother, and you decide you don't want to be like her at all, the last thing you want to do is to be so attentive to your child that you wind up becoming a smothering mother. It is indeed a very valid fear that you feel like your child might assume you do not care for him because you're not actively involved in every little thing that he does, but do remember your child also needs space. It's all about finding that sweet spot, where you give your child just enough attention, and just enough room to discover himself and do his own thing.

Were you hardly ever praised or acknowledged for your accomplishments when you were a child? Then understandably, you'll want to do things differently with your own kids. You might go to the other extreme, praising and encouraging your kids for every little thing, including successfully drawing air into their lungs. When you do this, you risk creating a situation where your child feels not only entitled, but also too much pressure to perform, so that they can consistently measure up to all the praise you shower them with. You might have your child feeling like a fraud because she doesn't quite feel like she is as awesome as you tell her. If your narcissistic mother was incredibly strict with you, don't be overly lenient with your child. Your child needs to understand that there are boundaries. Your child needs discipline, a guiding hand to help them know right from wrong. Yes, give her room to express herself. However, be sure to step in and step up when your child needs to learn why she should never do certain things. In the long run, it will save both you and your daughter a lot of headaches.

To be sure, it's really not easy to be a parent. I'd wager there is no such thing as the perfect parent. However, it does help to keep balance in mind when raising your kids, so you do not end up creating another dysfunctional dynamic in your relationship with them.

As You Are, So They Become

You need to also be mindful that as you find the sweet spot with your kids, you also serve as a model that would help them in the long run. You might find yourself acting from the assumption that you are simply not good enough. If you hold on to this belief, it will naturally show through your actions and words. Your children will then pick up on that, and grow to assume the same belief about themselves. You never need to say the words, "I don't believe I'm good enough." Children are very astute observers and will learn more from what you do than what you say.

If you never take care of yourself, or you remain in relationships and friendships which are not healthy, or you never go after your dreams, or you never take risks and prefer to stay safe and boring, your children will begin to emulate and imbibe all of that. However, if you do take great care of yourself, choose to go after what you want, stand up for yourself when you need to, and cut out toxic friendships and relationships, your kids will copy this as well.

Showing Empathy

As the daughter of a narcissistic mother, you never got any empathy growing up. As a result, you're not quite sure how to be empathetic towards your children. However, it's a skill worth learning, because there's nothing that could be more valuable to a child than a mother who hears him, understands him, and is able to support him because she can truly empathize with him.

The good news is that just because you never received empathy does not mean you cannot learn to be empathetic. Like a muscle, as you work it, it gets bigger and stronger. You need to be able to show empathy towards your children, so that in times of despair, you're able to connect with them and do right by them.

Get to Know the Little Person

Did you know, shocker of shockers, that your kid is actually a person you can get to know? It would appear most parents don't get that. They feel it's all about simply guiding the child, telling them what to do and what not to do, showing up for all the PTAs, giving them clothes, food, and shelter. There's a lot more to parenting. You can and should get to know your child!

If you're constantly going on about your child's achievements and not much else, then you might have a problem you're not even aware of. Your child does not feel like you know him. He feels like he exists only to keep you proud and happy about what he's done, and not much else. The thing you need to realize is that his successes do not equal who he is as a person.

What you get when you refuse to get in tune with this little person is that sooner or later they will give in to behaviors which are dangerous, because you've put her under so much pressure to succeed, and you don't seem to be open to conversations about who she really is, how she feels about things, and how she's doing. So rather than come to you to talk things over, she will find other ways to let go of the pressure — ways that are not necessarily healthy or legal. When you do find out, it always comes as a shock to you, because your child has mastered the fine art of showing you only what you want to see.

Authentic Emotions

You may completely agree that a child should be able to show their true feelings — that is, until you realize some of those feelings are not particularly positive, especially when it comes to you. When you realize this, please do not try to shut them down in any way. Do not refuse to hear them out, because then they will simply put on a face that they know you like, and everything real about your children will be hidden from you forever.

You may have learned as a child that you should never show your true emotions about anything. When you grow up with kids of your own, you may wonder how and why your children have become so problematic, despite you having done what you perceive to be your best. You may find yourself unwilling to confront them about their behavior because you really don't want to have to deal with the ugly truth, that somehow, you never let your kids express all their emotions, and so they've found ways to act out.

Please always be open to your kids expressing themselves. You should, because there have been countless instances where kids are going through things such as sexual abuse, but never say a word about it because they worry their parents won't believe them, or won't hear them out. When you encourage your kids to never show their authentic emotions, you might as well be a narcissist like your mother. It's unfair. Hear them out, and truly seek to understand them.

Burdening Your Kids

It's not an uncommon desire to want to be friends with your children. It's not unusual that you want to be very, very close to them. You never had any of that closeness with your mother, so naturally, you might desire it now. The thing is, though, that your daughter will always be your daughter. You will always be a mother, and so you are obligated to play that role. You're to give her guidance when your child needs it, show her empathy, and support her. This is not your daughter's duty to you. This is your duty to her.

Care for Yourself, Connect with Others

On the path to recovery as the daughter of a narcissistic mother, you do need to take care of yourself. This does not mean you should become self-centered, and neglect the needs and feelings of the people around you. Doing that is the complete antithesis of self-care and borders on narcissism. Remember how your mother was always all about herself? You don't want to become that person.

You will need to care for yourself if you hope to heal from the narcissistic wounds you carry about. However, this does not mean you should not give your children all the love, attention, and time they need. When you neglect your kids like this, it's not hard to get them to start acting out, finding new, creative ways to get in trouble at school or with the law.

If this happens with your children, understand that it's because they are angry and do not quite understand why you would neglect them like this. Make sure you stay in touch with your kids and help them understand that you're always available for them when they need you. Then you must follow through on that promise.

You might be wondering what it means to truly care for yourself in a way that is healthy for you and your family. It's really all about finding a way to feel fulfilled, so that you've got all the love, time, energy, attention, and empathy that your family will need from you. It all ties back in to finding the perfect balance — that sweet spot we talked about. You need to realize that there are shades of gray, and nothing is an either-or case.

The "Special" Relationship between Narcissistic Mothers and Their Daughters

In a perfect world, your mother is supposed to be the first person you fall in love with, because she is essentially the one who ushers you into this world. She is the one who nurtures you, supports you, and helps you discover yourself, as well as navigate your way through life and living. She is the one who makes you feel comfortable and secure. You learn about everything you need to know through her. You long for her to hold you, touch you, smile with you, and be there always. The way she treats you and how empathetic she is with you dictate what you feel and desire, and also help you understand your place in the world and how much you matter and are valued.

The narcissistic mother is very incapable of empathy, and as a result, she completely wrecks the development of her child on a psychological level. All she ever sees in the child is her own reflection, and nothing more. As a result, she has no sense of boundaries. She is blissfully unaware of the distinct separation between herself and those who call her mother. She does not realize that her own children are actually distinct individuals, all unique in their own way, and all very deserving of her love and affection. No matter how the signs and symptoms of narcissistic personality disorder vary, one thing that stays constant is that the narcissist is the worst when it comes to parenting.

I should make it clear that the effects of having a narcissistic mother differ when it comes to sons and daughters. More often than not, the girls will spend a lot more time with their mothers than the sons, and as a result they would look up to their mothers as role models.

The narcissistic mother will always think of her daughter as not just a threat, but also as a subordinate extension to herself. She'll make use of the twin blades of criticism and control so she can mold her daughter into a more acceptable version — usually into the person that she wishes she could become. While doing this, she will also project a lot onto her daughter — including the terrible, unlovable things about herself. She will project her own coldness, self-centeredness, and cruelty, among other things. It does not stop there. She will also project her own mother's perceived shortcomings onto her daughter as well. You might also notice that the narcissistic mother has a preference for her male children. This doesn't mean you should envy the boys. To be sure, they go through their own fair share of abuse from the narcissistic mother, and being expected to provide the kind of support that they could not possibly provide as kids. This is known as emotional incest.

The relationship between the narcissistic mother and her daughter involves a lot of shame in order to establish control, and force the daughter to never quite learn who her true self is. As a result of the shame and inability to find her authentic voice, the daughter becomes very insecure, unable to trust her gut or her head. She also assumes responsibility for her mother's displeasure, thinking she must be broken in some way or doing things wrong. She has no idea that her mother will simply never find anything she says or does to be enough to warrant love or empathy. Sometimes, things get so dark that the daughter of a narcissistic mother will feel as though she simply should not be in existence. This comes as a result of her mother constantly treating her like an unwanted burden which she would rather have aborted when she had the chance.

While some narcissistic mothers will do their best to lie about abusing their daughter, and go as far as they need to hide the signs, there are those who don't even need to pretend, since they're married to men who are too passive to shield their daughters from the abuse, or may even take part in the abuse. The daughter learns over time not to bother protecting herself, and not to bother standing up for her own rights. She grows accustomed to being and feeling defenseless, so much so that in her adult years, she does not even realize when she is being mistreated by others. The narcissistic mother teaches her daughter to feel ashamed all the time. She teaches her to be ashamed of everything about herself. So, this daughter goes about feeling like she could never possibly be loved or accepted the way she truly is. She finds herself always having to make a choice between putting one more nail in the coffin where her authentic self lies, or setting that true self free while damning herself to never receiving her mother's love. When she grows up, she finds herself in codependent relationships, constantly feeling the strain of denying herself and making room for others while she shrinks into nothingness. Since her mother rejected her authentic self, she also rejects it.

As a result, the daughter of a narcissistic mother finds that she has this deep-rooted shame that she just can't let go of. She feels ashamed that her authentic self could never ever be loved. How could it ever be? Her very own mother could not find it in herself to love her for who she truly is. She could not accept her own daughter, so who else could find it in themselves to accept her? No one thinks about the poor daughter. Beyond just the shame, there's the anger, loathing, and resentment that the daughter feels towards her narcissistic mother. She can't quite explain why she feels this way. This adds to the feeling of guilt and shame that she carries around. The only reason she must hate her mother is because as her mother has told her and showed her over and over, she really is a terrible person. Her mother's harsh criticisms must definitely have some truth to them, thinks the daughter. She grows up feeling less than, never good enough for good things or good people. She grows up thinking you must earn love and friendship. It can't possibly be freely given, in her eyes. As a result, she constantly has to deal with abandonment issues in her grown-up relationships.

Narcissistic mothers might take a moment to care for their daughter's needs. That's where the care ends. As the daughter of a narcissistic mother, you find that your emotional needs are not even acknowledged. There's no form of closeness between you and your mother. There's none of the tender care that a mother should provide her daughter. So, you end up constantly feeling like something is missing, though you cannot say what. You crave understanding and warmth from the woman who bore you, but you never get it.

What you'll find is that there is zero connection between you and your narc of a mother. You have no idea what you need emotionally, or that your emotional needs are valid and should be tended to. You have no idea where to begin to nurture yourself emotionally, or to give yourself the comfort that you never got. You may seek out relationships and friendships with others to fill this hole on the inside, but more often than not, you find yourself facing the same thing you did with your mother, over and over again.

Growing up with your mother, you found that she only ever cared about herself. She never gave a damn about what you needed, how you felt, or who you were as a person. She would do her best to control all these things for you, so that your true desires were buried forever, unacknowledged not just by her but by you as well. There was only ever one way to exist for you, and it was your mother's. Such narcissistic mothers pay more attention to themselves, or at best their male children, but never to you, her daughter.

Your narcissistic mother would dictate to you how you should look and behave, not giving a fig about how you'd prefer to be. She would criticize you until you were left with no option than to yield. She chooses your outfits, your food, your work, even your lovers. It's always under the guise of it all being "for your own benefit." She would always undermine your decisions so that you learned to never trust your own discernment. The daughter of a narcissistic mother will find herself in unfair and unreasonable competition with her mother when it comes to things like her own children's love, or her husband's love. She'll do anything and everything to keep the spotlight on her, not you. She has got to be the prettiest, the nicest, most loving and loved one. Not you. While she insists that your significant other is no good for you, the narcissistic mother will nevertheless throw herself at your own boyfriend or girlfriend. If she is going to remain numero uno in your life, then she sees it as her duty to undermine every single relationship of yours.

I've just painted you a picture of the relationship between most daughters and their narcissistic mothers. It's not pretty at all, and the trauma of it all can leave you with some very nasty emotional and mental scars. I promise you that you can recover from it all. You can recover from the shame and rejection you deal with. It will take some time and a good bit of effort, but you can. It means you will also be able to break up with codependency.

The road to healing involves a clear understanding that all the things your mother said to make you feel so ashamed of yourself are baseless and far from the truth. Then you'll need to fire that negative voice in your head — your mother's — and in its place, create a new voice that continues to nurture you, support you, and love you. Self-love is key, if you're going to heal.

Chapter 5 - Effects of Being Raised by a Narcissistic Parent

If you were raised by a narcissist, it is going to directly affect the way that you are acting now. Some individuals might even grow fearful that they have become narcissists themselves. Though this is possible, you have to remember that we will usually just have the side effects of this lifestyle rather than the actual toxic thoughts that a narcissist usually has.

The Ways Manipulation Has Occurred

As we grew up, many children of narcissistic moms dealt with constant criticism, judgment, and harsh feedback on every little thing you did. Did you have someone standing over your shoulder watching as you cooked, cleaned, or did anything else around the house? It was always a hard challenge in some people's homes because they would be told to do something, like clean up the house, but as they did, they would end up getting judged the entire time. It was like you were at fault for not doing it, but then when you did do it, someone was there to give you negative feedback right away. There were often many situations in which neither person could really win in the end.

This was a form of manipulation. It occurred throughout small instances, but after months and months of negativity spewing from the narcissistic parent's mouth, it became the way that their children thought. These manipulation tactics gave the narcissist the upper hand. When there was a confrontation, even one where the narcissist might have been blatantly wrong, the abused would still consider themselves at fault because they had been so manipulated by the abuser. They struggle to really understand their thoughts and are constantly judging themselves because of what the narcissistic mom might have said to them in the beginning. Another form of manipulation that happened over time was the constant pretending of not knowing what the truth of the situation was. Narcissistic mothers are more passive in their abuse than some fathers. There aren't many statistics to really show us verbal versus physical abuse among fathers and mothers, but when discussing narcissism with mothers or reading experiences online, it's common that the mother was more passive. One of her tricks is to use ignorance to pretend as though nothing is wrong. There are some instances where the mother might even allow abuse to happen from the father and pretend as though they aren't aware of just how bad it is. This ignorance is first a way to disconnect from reality. The narcissist doesn't acknowledge their faults and admit they're wrong easily. They will instead do whatever they have to in order to validate their own perspective. If something is blatantly staring at them, right in their direct eye path, they'll come up with an excuse like, "Oh, I was looking at the ground." These excuses don't make any sense, but it is the kind of manipulation that can make us feel as though we're crazy throughout our lives.

The biggest way that we have been manipulated over time is through the use of blaming us. Children are NEVER to blame for their parent's issues. Children are not scapegoats. They are not at fault for their presence. The older we get, the more in charge we are of our emotions, and though we might have gone through terrible things in our childhood, we're still able to make certain choices. However, if you look back on your life before the time when you were ten, twelve, fourteen, and so on, you were still just a kid. Even a parent kicking their child out at sixteen is extreme. Some people think that you aren't a child at this point, but our brains really don't stop developing until our mid-twenties. Some teens are more responsible than others; however, a narcissistic mother kicking their child out isn't healthy, and yet, many people will still end up blaming themselves for instances like this.

How a Narcissist Influences Your Mindset

All of these manipulation tactics that we discussed will get into your head. It is almost like you become brainwashed. Not all cases are as extreme as the methods of brainwashing that we know to be true; however, you will often still hear the voice of your narcissistic mother in the back of your head. Perhaps you are picking out clothing, getting a haircut, or decorating your home. You might end up hearing their judgments in the background. Maybe something bad happened and you feel bad about yourself. Perhaps you still hear your mother's voice judging you and affirming that you did something wrong. It is very normal to hear the voice of your abuser in your head even in moments where you really just want them to go away.

When you start to have feelings surface, you might try to stuff them right back down. A narcissist doesn't like talking about anyone's feelings other than their own. It becomes normalized to simply ignore any emotion that you have. Rather than looking at your own feelings, you might end up taking on the feelings of others. If there is a situation where multiple people are upset, rather than taking care of yourself, you might simply try to play caretaker for everyone else.

Ignoring your needs is very normal for those who have become free from narcissistic parental abuse by their mother. At the same time, you might still feel these emotions very intensely, only they don't come out in the right way. In one instance, you might have formed severe depression because of what you were always told about yourself. Perhaps you were made to feel as though you have no value, you are worthless, you aren't good enough, and that you can't do anything right. This is very invalidating and in the end, you might believe that it is so true that you even harm yourself because of these challenging emotions. You could also end up falling into a pit of despair where you can't do anything at all, you have trouble making decisions, and even simple tasks like doing the dishes or showering is a struggle. Constant thoughts of your unworthiness might fester within you, making it difficult to basically exist.

On the other hand, this could have turned into anger. You might feel anger at your mother, anger at yourself, and anger at the world for allowing this abuse to happen. In the end, you could end up lashing out at people or internalizing that anger and growing hate for yourself. The lack of justice that you felt from this could create feelings of hopelessness.

No matter what you feel now, understand that your mindset has been influenced. In a two year or less romantic relationship with a narcissist, there are going to be wounds which need to heal. However, spending 18 years of your developing life with a narcissist means that you are going to have to continually check in with your thoughts and remind yourself that not everything you think was created on your own; it's frequently the voice of your abuser still latching on.

The Emotional Roller Coaster Created

Living with a narcissist means going on an emotional roller coaster. There are ups and downs, and no matter what you try to do, you will always be strapped in along for the ride, unable to really break out of this toxic cycle. A narcissistic roller coaster starts with that good feeling first. There are happy emotions. Everything is OK! You're getting along. You're excited about what's going to happen. You are building a healthy relationship and they seem to be love bombing you. This phase is more apparent in romantic relationships that have just started. For example, let's say that there is a boyfriend and girlfriend, the boy being the narcissist. He has chosen a girl to pursue based on the fact that she's sweet, caring, and emotional. They hit it off and they start the love-bombing phase. He tells her everything that she wants to hear. He's there to help her through her darkest times. He's going to take care of her for the rest of his life and nothing bad will ever happen, right? He showers her with gifts and attention to the point that she can't see any of the red flags along the way because everything is going to get better now!

This is more complex in a parent-child relationship because you're with them from the moment that you're born. You don't have that initial meeting period where you get to know them. You don't really have the chance to escape before it's too late. Even if red flags are there, you won't be able to spot them, especially as someone who's four, seven, twelve, and so on. This love-bombing period likely comes during a different life event. Maybe they got a new job. Perhaps they finally quit drinking. A new house, marriage, and other life events could be the start of this roller coaster where you feel like things are good and everything is going to be happy as it should be.

This is all as you're rising up the roller coaster. Then you make it to the top, and things start to get ugly. There's the initial drop, where there might be an explosive fight, a freak-out instance, a nasty altercation, and so on. Suddenly, everything is terrible as it was just before this new change occurred. Once you have worked through this, then things could potentially drop even worse. There might also be a slight chance of a smaller hill that you go up. Maybe they say they're sorry. They acknowledge what they did and apologize. However, this becomes meaningless because they end up doing the exact same thing over again. In some instances, there is the moment where everyone is just gone. Maybe they don't talk to you, give you the silent treatment, and you simply don't hear from them. This is like the end of the roller coaster where you're just waiting to get off. The only thing is, in the end, you're not sure if you're going to end up being able to get off or if you're just going to have to ride the roller coaster over again.

Self-Blame

Child abuse, in all forms, will eventually lead to periods of self-blame. What does this mean? As we've touched on a bit, you will often feel responsible not only for your parent's suffering but the things that happened to you as well. Though you were an innocent child with no control over how others might treat you, at the end of the day, you're still the one that can end up feeling the weight of all the abuse that you've experienced. This leads to a damaged self-image and constant feelings of regret and remorse. You might frequently have ruminating thoughts, endless guilt, and even PTSD from what it is that you experienced. Feeling regret isn't always a bad thing. It can lead to us looking back on our lives and taking responsibility for the mistakes that we might have made. The thing is, you didn't do anything wrong as a child of abuse. You didn't have any choice in whether these would be your parents. You weren't given the opportunity to fully feel the things that you did and express them in a healthy way.

We have to consider how fragile a child's mind will be. Children don't see the world through empathetic eyes. We are a bit more selfish as we age because that is how the mind begins. We only look out for ourselves and ensure that our basic needs are met. Because of this, it creates a more egotistical view of the world. We are considering things through our own eyes. This means that we can end up taking responsibility for things that are out of our control. As a child, you probably looked at your parent's fight as something that you did wrong. If your mom was struggling, maybe you took the blame.

You were a child that was just trying to understand. You weren't taught the reality of the situation, so you end up only being able to take a child-like perception away from this. It becomes something that you had control over, and you'll feel guilty that you lost your ability to take care of the situation in a way that you thought it could have been handled.

You might end up constantly criticizing yourself, thinking that you should have done better in other areas that you have control over. It's easier to label things as either positive or negative because that's the only control that you've ever had. Your ability to reason can be skewed as you grow because you weren't given the chance to fully develop. This means that down the line, you'll end up not having a clear perspective, so labeling things is the way that you reason. This creates an "all-or-nothing" kind of perspective. It will make you doubt yourself, and you might even get to the point where you hurt yourself. Your relationships can become damaged, and you might experience frequent anxiety. This can all stem simply because you don't know how to not blame yourself for the things that your narcissistic parents might have done to you.

Unrealistic Self-Appraisal

In the same way that you criticize yourself endlessly, you might also discover that you are overinflating your own ego in some instances. A narcissistic parent can be great at building us up while also tearing us down in the same breath. They can say something like, "You're more beautiful than anyone else in school. If only you were as smart." They manage to find a way to compliment you and make you feel better than anything else, but they are also perfect at cutting you right where it hurts the most. This creates a very skewed perception of reality, and you will often struggle to determine what the truth is versus what you are just taught to believe.

The issue with this is that we either think that we are terrible people or that we are better than everyone else. Did you get a good grade on your test? You must be smarter than the rest of your classmates. Did you fail? You're the dumbest person to ever walk the planet. This switch between our perspectives is not healthy. It's just one test, not the defining moment of your life. Did you make a cake that everyone enjoyed? You're a talented chef. Did you drop that cake? You ruined the party and the rest of the year as well. This is so not the case! We can't allow ourselves to think in such extreme ways because it is like a teetering seesaw that is bound to shoot us like a cannon into the air when one side drops. If you hold yourself in such high esteem, this means that you will feel even worse when something terrible does happen.

We have to recognize ourselves as the balanced individuals that we are. We are both good and bad in some instances. That doesn't make us terrible people that don't deserve good things. Should you have started that project sooner? Probably. Does this make you a bad person? Absolutely not. Did you help a friend out when they moved into their place? This makes you a good friend, but it doesn't mean that you are a better friend than anyone else and you deserve special treatment. Sometimes that inflated sense of self comes from our parents. They might have always talked you up and projected their narcissistic qualities onto you. They might have compared you in a positive light and built your ego over others because they were making themselves feel more validated in the process.

You deserve to feel good about yourself! You should be proud of your accomplishments! We just have to ensure that we are holding ourselves at the same level that we hold other people. If someone else did the same thing, would you judge them in a similar manner that you do yourself? This is what we'll have to continually ask ourselves in the process of healing.

Poor Self-Discipline

Because we weren't able to regulate our emotions as children, this will directly affect our ability to have self-discipline. Self-discipline doesn't mean that you're hard on yourself and always criticizing your actions. Those who have a high level of discipline know what they need to get done, know what they want in the end, and have a great action plan for getting those things.

The reason that we struggle with self-discipline is usually because our emotions aren't regulated. It's important that we learn how to separate our emotions from the reactions that we have. For example, you might discover that you are an emotional eater. Every time you get into a fight with your mom, you go to the freezer to grab some ice cream or to the pantry for some chips. It might lead you to gain some weight. You then start to blame yourself for not having any self-discipline. Why can't you just say no to the chips?

The reason that you struggle with this isn't because you don't have the discipline needed to get what you want. You are simply not able to control your own emotions. You're struggling to recognize and regulate your feelings; therefore, you are going to continue to act impulsively. The problem isn't with you and your personality. It is that you were never given proper lessons on controlling your feelings and working through them when you need to.

Perhaps you have a temper and you can't help but lash out at people when you get upset. You weren't just born angry. You were never taught to separate your emotion from your reaction. Your emotion, the anger, the sadness that causes you to eat, the frustration, and the guilt are all very valid feelings. You are perfectly normal for having them and the thoughts that they might bring along. Where it gets tricky is when you use these feelings to have an impulsive action. The anger is real and valid – punching a wall because of it is not.

Anger Towards Yourself

You often can't take the anger out on the other person, so it's easier to just take it out on yourself. If you did ever express your emotions in the past, you might have had to keep them bottled up thereafter because you were punished for saying something. We're frequently taught that violence is bad as well. If you can't express your feelings on other people, then the only thing that we think we have the option to do in the end is to take that anger out on ourselves.

Anger is an important topic that we need to discuss, especially in sons of narcissistic mothers. It is a stereotype to believe that men are more likely to be angry than women, but we can't overlook the fact that this might still be a huge part for you in your recovery from the emotional abuse. As children, we don't get to be angry at our parents. They tell us to improve our attitude or make us feel guilty for having that feeling in the first place. we certainly aren't always in control of the anger we feel, and rather than being taught how to properly manage it, we are instead told that we need to stuff it down inside.

What happens is that this anger doesn't go away. Imagine shaking up a bottle of soda. If you shake it too hard, it can end up exploding. If you shake it just hard enough, throughout time, it won't explode. However, once you finally do open it up, it is going to be a lot different than it was in the first place. If you take this anger and do nothing with it, you can end up letting it become something that destroys you.

When you are angry, you have a loss of your emotions. Anger is a secondary response to an emotion that is there in the first place. Depression, anxiety, stress, and other mental health disorders might even play a role in the way that you are finding anger coming into your life. We aren't given the tools needed to understand and express our emotions. In this way, we do what we can on our own to try and control these feelings. Anger can make you feel like you are powerless, and that's not something that ever feels good.

If you yell at your friend or partner, it can feel like you gained power for a moment. You certainly grab their attention and they are finally willing to listen to you. This is why many individuals will yell frequently when they are angry. They need to gain that sense of power back. Then there are those that will take their anger out on objects. Is your TV remote not working? It can help to slam it on the coffee table, right? That makes it work? This is wrong as well. It just inflates your anger and isn't addressing the reality of the situation. Still, hitting the remote can give you that feeling like you do have control over it, so in the end, it becomes easier to try and gain a sense of power over the emotions that make us feel powerless.

Finally, anger might make you take things out on yourself. You might self-medicate through alcohol, cut different parts of your body, or deprive yourself of things that you need, like food, or even just having fun in general. When you are angry, you can turn that inwards and self-harm because it makes you feel in control. You are the one in charge of punishing yourself. When you have experienced pain so frequently from other people. it makes you feel good to inflict the pain on yourself because finally, you are in control instead of others who have had the power in the past. At the same time, self-harm can also make us feel as though we have responsibility and that we can take care of ourselves. Maybe you physically harm yourself, only to tend to your bruises afterwards. Perhaps you binge eat but purge through laxatives or vomiting afterwards. You are inflicting the pain yourself and then you are taking care of it yourself, and this can make us feel very accomplished with a higher self-esteem. If you don't manage your anger, it means not managing this part of your emotions as well.

Counterdependency
We briefly discussed codependency and how this can affect your relationship. Let's take a further look now at what counterdependency is and how you might have experienced this.
When you're dependent on other people, you often put your trust into them. It might be low self-esteem or even a feeling of having no control that might cause a person to be dependent on someone else. They like to put fate into the hands of others because it's easier than accepting that they have a responsibility over themselves. When we aren't trusting of our own decisions and feel incapable of making certain choices, it's really easy to hope that another person is going to be able to make the right choices for us.
Then there is counterdependency. This is when you don't trust others at all. There is sometimes a bond breakage in a child's life where they can

no longer emotionally depend on another person. Whether it's because they're not close with this individual, or they've been moved around so frequently that they can't depend on any steady adult, a child can lose their faith in other caregivers as they age. As the child of a narcissistic mother, it's likely that at some point in your life, you gave up on depending on other people.

You'll see many with "trust no one" spread across their social media or even tattooed on their body. While it's true that there are plenty of people in this world whom we cannot depend on, we have to remember that it's also not healthy to completely avoid relying on others to the point that it affects our lives. You might not trust someone to decorate your home for you, but it would be unhealthy to not be able to trust someone to even be in your home. It's OK to not trust someone to wash your mother's antique wedding china while doing the dishes, but not having faith in someone to do the dishes at all could be a sign that you have certain trust issues.

It's important to be a healthy, independent individual. We should all have a certain level of autonomy in which we recognize our own abilities and improve on them in a healthy way. We choose to be independent because it means that we are living to our fullest potential. At the same time, a healthy autonomous person also understands that they have to be willing to put some trust into others, and that they won't always be capable of doing everything on their own.

If you are counterdependent, it might mean that you always feel the need to be right. Even when you're wrong, you have to look for a way that you were right or at least misunderstood, because if not, it might hurt your ego. In the same instance, it can be difficult creating strong relationships and being close to others. You might have never had that close relationship with someone where the two of you can depend on each other, so now, it's hard for you to know what trust in a relationship even looks like.

This trait can bring up some narcissistic qualities such as being more self-centered or having an egotistical personality. You might also have trouble asking for help even when you need it. Asking for help might mean that you appear vulnerable or weak (in some people's eyes), which is something that counterdependents don't want others to see.

After considering these qualities, you might even ask yourself, "Am I a narcissist?" This can be one of the narcissistic victim's biggest fears, so let's discover that if this could even be the case with you now.

Chapter 6 - Mental Manipulation and Control

Manipulation refers to the use of indirect tactics to control a certain behavior, relationship, and emotions. Manipulation is actually trying to get someone to do something that they don't want to do, then making sure that they end up doing what you want.

Manipulation can be both positive and negative. You might manipulate someone to do what you want for the benefit of both of you or manipulate them to do something that isn't beneficial to them, only for your benefits.

In narcissistic relationships, manipulation has a lot of consequences, and it is usually associated with a lot of emotional abuse, especially when you share a tight bond with the other person. Many people look at manipulation in a negative way, especially when it hurts the emotional and mental health of the person that is being manipulated.

A Narcissist will manipulate you so that they are in total control of the environment and the surroundings that you live in. the urge to manipulate you stems from the fact that they have a deep form of anxiety or fear that they can't work with. When you are the victim of manipulation, you will experience a wide range of effects.

Why Do Mothers Manipulate?

There are many reasons why a narcissistic mother chooses to manipulate the kids. The reasons will, however, vary from one person to the next. However, there are a few reasons why people end up manipulating others, and these include:

They feel worthless, helpless, and hopeless.

They have the fear that their kids will abandon them.

They have the innate need for control and power over other people.

They have the willingness to use their feelings in front of the needs of others.

The need to raise their self-esteem.

Signs of Manipulative Mothers

1. They Prey on Your Weaknesses

People that manipulate others have mastered deception to a very high level. They will appear sincere and respectable in their dealings, but deep within them, it is just a façade. It is a way to draw you in so that you will be in a relationship or you will do something for them before they show their true colors.

The manipulative mother isn't genuinely interested in you as a person rather than the vehicle that will allow her to gain control so that you become an object in their many games.

They have several ways that they do this, for instance, they will grab anything you say or do then will twist it around so that it is not in any way recognizable to you. They will try to complicate issues and will confuse you, even make it feel like you are the crazy one in any relationship.

They will change the truth around and will resort to lies if it serves their beliefs and helps them get their needs.

They will also try to be the victim when, in reality, you are the one affected. The aim is to try and paint you in a negative picture so that they stay in the limelight. If they are the ones that caused a problem, they will not be there to take any responsibility for it; rather will prey on your fears and insecurities.

One of the techniques is to make you defensive. They threaten and bully you so that you can submit to their world of thought.

Here are the top traits of manipulative people; so that you can know what to watch for in case one comes along.

2. They Lack Insight

Manipulative mothers don't know how to engage with people, and to this end, they create certain scenarios that will absolve them of any responsibility. They believe that the only way to handle a situation between them, you or their husband is to make sure their needs are met. This is all that matters in the relationship with other people.

Basically, all the situations and anything else is about what they will feel, what they want, and what other people think about them. What other people feel doesn't matter at all.

They don't have the time to question themselves so that they can know what the issue is; instead, they only see the problem to be someone else.

3. They Don't Give in To Boundaries

Manipulative mothers don't know what a boundary is. They will go after what they want without any regard to who gets hurt when they go for their goals. They will crowd your space in all ways without little or no concern over what you feel.

They don't know what you need your space, and they will tell you that they don't care what you do or how you do it, as long as you give in to their needs.

When they are always in your space, they will end up weakening you, demeaning you, depleting your energy and even making you fail.

4. Always Blaming Others

Manipulative mothers avoid any responsibilities that come their way by blaming others for causing the issue. They understand clearly what manipulation is, but they just don't see anything wrong with putting the responsibility on someone else.

They get satisfaction when you take up the responsibility that was meant to be theirs. They will try to use the responsibility to satisfy their needs and leave no room for you to fulfill yours.

5. Are Predators

A predator is someone that preys on your vulnerabilities at all times. Manipulative mothers will prey on any weakness that you have – emotional sensitivity and anything that they can get a hold on that they know will make you bow to their orders.

They know that you have a kind heart, so they will use this to make you do what they want.

They might go after your kindness and goodness at first, praising you for the wonderful person that you are. But this is all about getting you into their web of deceit. Over time, the praises will reduce because they just want to use you then let you go. They don't care so much about you – what they care about is what you can do for them to make them happy.

6. They Talk Ill About Others

If you want to know the real intention of the Manipulative mother, and then pay attention to the way they talk about other people in relation to what you do for them. What they tell you about other people is what they will tell others about you.

They have mastered the art of "triangulation, whereby they come up with various scenarios and then create an environment of jealousy, rivalry and create a lot of disharmonies.

7. They Invite You to their "Space"

One of the biggest signs of a master manipulator is that they find a way to get you to their space so that they can' take control of the situation. The mother might have come up with a personal space that they feel they have total control of; this might be their bedroom or the kitchen.

The persona space for a manipulator is usually away from other people that might interfere in the process of manipulating you. Their comfort zone will make you feel like a stranger, even when it is a home that you have lived in for many years, and you won't be able to speak up against her.

8. They Pretend to Listen

You will at first think that she is a very good listener and see it as good behavior, but what they are after is looking for loopholes in what you are saying so that they can discredit you. They look for the holes so that they can find something to criticize you, and then judge you just to fulfill their egos.

They will let you talk from start to finish all day and then turn around and use this information against you. They can even be up any secret that you shared with them in front of other people.

9. They Exaggerate

Manipulative mothers will find a way to turn around the truth so that it works in their favor. Even when you realize that they have turned around the truth, they will brush it off in a ginger way and come up with hidden truths in the same words that you said.

They will take what you said and look for a few words that will make the same seem like a half-truth. If you decide to challenge them, they will twist the truth and paint you in a negative manner.

To confuse you further, they will often make use of a lot of information so that you don't know how and when to respond. The aim is to make you feel so overwhelmed that you cannot process the information overload.

As a result, they end up making the decision for you and all you have to do to go along with what they say or do.

10. They Block You

This is especially common when you are doing something with your mother at home. Let us say that you have gone to the supermarket to get a few items for dinner, and you arrive there and whenever you request for something she blocks you. The aim isn't even about a lack f money, but she just wants to show you that she is the one in control and you have nothing to do. She will give you so many roadblocks so that you are too frustrated to succumb to what the mother wants.

11. They Are Loud

For some reason, Manipulative mothers think that if they talk in a loud voice, they will sound smarter than anyone else in the room. They also always think that talking louder makes them look smart in front of other people. They do this all the time. Do you remember when you went for an event, and your mother was the loudest in the room till you became embarrassed?

The loudness is all about trying to push you into submission. You will never be successful if you engage in a shouting match with your narcissistic mother.

Even when you try to interject, they just keep on talking, with no regard about what you are trying to say. They will accompany the talks with a lot of aggressive body movements. They will talk louder so that they can gain control over everyone else in the room. You have no choice but to hear them out.

12. Always Negative

Manipulative mothers aren't happy people, and this reflects through both life and work. They will yell and scream at all people, regardless of their age and status. They might also decide to go silent, and in all this, they are enjoying immensely.

It is because they are unhappy that they want everyone else to share in their unhappiness. When other people are unhappy, they see that they are in full control of the situation, but what they do just ruins the environment for everyone.

13. They Have Conditions

They will give you a condition that you have to fulfill in order to get in their good books. If they give you a task in the home, they will order you to take it or to leave it, which will please them because they know you are working under their orders.

They are good at what they do, and when they give orders, you won't know whether it is a bluff or it isn't.

It might be very tricky, and when the manipulator is your mother, you won't realize that they are setting you up to fail.

14. They Ridicule You

Manipulative mothers will find any situation to make you feel bad about yourself over something that you have done or accomplished. They will do this in such a way that it isn't as obvious to all people but just you. The Manipulative mother knows your weak spots and goes for them. And when she does, she will hit it really hard so that you don't have what it takes to hit back.

The negative comment might be something as simple as commenting on your way of dressing, but from experience, you know that they are out to hurt you.

15. They Judge Openly

Manipulative mothers make no apologies when you get offended, and in most cases will not apologize for saying that they are wrong or they have done something wrong. It might not be the wrong thing for you, but as long as it doesn't please her, then it is wrong in her sight.

If you don't do things the right way according to her, then you will always be wrong.

They get the thrill when they know that they have embarrassed you, and this shows other people that they have the power over you at all times.

16. The Feast on Convenient Friendship

Have you met a person that doesn't give you the time of day but when you offer something that they want they will be all friendly to you?

You might not have thought about this fact before, but when you look at it closely, it is a sure sign of emotional manipulation.

Manipulative mothers will try to get close to you just because they need something from you at that time, not because they need your company. They are selfish and will stop at nothing to make sure they get what they want – even if it means using you to their own selfish interests.

17. They Make You Question Your Abilities

Manipulative mothers will have the expertise to make you doubt your capabilities. They will make you feel silly for doing and saying things, even if they are important to you. They will also make your feelings seem unimportant at all times.

18. Little or No Time to Decide

When the manipulative mother has already come up with a decision that you need to follow, they will give you very little time to decide. She will apply tension and total control over you so that you don't have the capacity to say no or yes – you will just accept the decision she makes on your behalf.

19. Denying Past Promises

A person that tries to manipulate you will give you a lot of promises just to get you to do something. However, these promises never mature, and you will never get what you were promised. You will follow up on the promises so much that you will end up being frustrated.

When you try to remind the person that she promised you anything, you will get rebuffed, and the situation will be turned back on you. They swear that when they promised whatever it is they did, you were not keen and you didn't understand whatever they said. They will always brand you to be forgetful or crazy.

When this happens, you will question your memories and your resolves.

20. Guilt Tripping

A narcissistic mother is a queen of being the perfect victim. Rather than being in aggressive behavior, the mother will become passive-aggressive. They will come up with guilty trips just to try and make you feel bad about yourself.

21. They Ignore Your Problems

Rather than being empathetic when you have an issue, they tend to make it their own. If you are sick, they will come up with the same issue that you have but worse. If you fight with your sibling, they will find a way to turn it around so that they make you look bad in it.

Once the mother manipulates you, the effects can be short or long term.

Effects of Emotional Manipulation

When it comes to emotional manipulation by a narcissistic mother, you won't see the physical effects. The scars that come from the manipulation aren't physical; rather, they affect the emotional well-being of the person for years to come.

Short Term Effects:

These occur within the period of manipulation and include:

Surprise and Confusion

Mental manipulation makes you feel that what is happening doesn't need to be so. You will be wondering whether the person that you have known to be the mother you love is behaving like a stranger to you.

Questioning Yourself

You will start wondering if you remember the things that you did before because the person will keep on making it seem as if you have a problem. This is because everything and anything that you say or do will be questioned. Narcissistic mothers will also tell you that the memory you have about something is wrong all the time.

Anxiety

For you to avoid any future manipulation, you might become anxious when something tries to repeat itself in the same way it happened before. You will try to avoid behavior that might lead to the same outcomes as before, or look for behavior that points to an outburst.

Passiveness

You know that when you react to a situation, it will lead to more pain and a relationship that is emotionally abusive. Due to this, you decide to be passive so that you don't make things go the same way they did before.

This starts as a defensive technique that, with time becomes something that you develop into a habit.

Shame

You will find yourself putting a lot of blame on yourself for things that have happened before, even when you are not involved. When they blame you, it becomes harder to prevent yourself from taking it out on yourself and the people around you.

Long Term Effects:

Isolation

When you become oppressed by a narcissistic mother, you tend to become more of an observer rather than a person that acts. You will end up feeling nothing at all towards situations that ought to make you happy. In the end, you feel damaged and hopeless and unable to feel the emotions again.

Always Asking for Approval

Since you have seen the manifestation of anger in your own mother over and over again, you will keep on asking for approval for the things that need to come naturally to you. You start aiming to please people all the time, and this makes you a beggar in situations that are in your own right. Since you have been made to believe that you aren't perfect all the time, you decide to make yourself seem perfect so that other people can appreciate you.

You Become Resentful

When you have gone through so much till you don't have what it takes to make your own decisions, you will show this in the form of impatience, irritability, and frustration. When you become resentful, you develop frustrations, and you become impatient, irritable, and you keep on blaming yourself all the time.

After you are treated badly by a narcissistic mother, you will not have anything good to say about anything that relates to the situation.

Judgmental

You will find yourself looking out for what other people are doing or saying at all times. You will expect a lot from people so that the excessive expectations end up frustrating you more. This is a way of trying to be in control all the time after you have never been in control for a long time.

Depression

Following emotional abuse and manipulation, you will find that there are so many lies that you have been told that were never true. The good news is that depression can be easily healed over time.

Control Tactics of Narcissistic Mothers

The narcissistic mother uses various control tactics that will make you do what she wants without a lot of questions.

Mind control is a method where the mother uses a lot of manipulative tactics to affect your behaviors and brain function.

Here are a few methods that the narcissistic mother ill-use frequently to get to you:

Emotional Appeal

The narcissistic mother will try to plan on your emotions such as guilt, fear, and loyalty rather than reasoning and logic.

They use their emotional appeal in such a way that they come up with outrageous claims towards you. They use emotions to control others so that it comes naturally to them.

Bandwagon Effect

The narcissistic mother will try and make you go along with other things just because other people are doing it. They understand the power of numbers and will follow others with the aim of getting the right attention. For instance, they will desire a lot of followers on social media so that they can get their thrill on. They often make use of group thinking to play on the fears of other people.

They will make it seem that other people are agreeing with her so that she can make you do something for her. If other people are buying a particular item, she will tell you how "everyone has it" so that she can cajole you into picking up the item.

Only Two Options

The narcissistic mother will give you only two options – either you do this or…

They view the world in just two options that you have to choose from, they will get their comfort from the two choices, and they will force you to choose from the two so that they have some power over you.

False Flattery

They will butter you up so that when they ask for anything, you will be more receptive to their needs. They will pile you with compliments that don't make sense only for them to get what they want, and then they show their true colors.

They will try all they can to get what they want, and then they will leave once they get what they want.

Incredulity

They act as if what you have done is very unbelievable. They usually use the tactic when they don't get what the other person is saying. Rather than admit that they don't get what you are saying, they will pretend that what you are saying or doing is beyond belief at all times.

This is usually common when you have a valid concern, and yet the other person wishes to rubbish them. The narcissistic mother will take up a stance that will make you feel as if you are saying a lie.

They Label You

The narcissistic mother will apply negative labels to their kids. These labels are single words that will humiliate you and make you feel as if you are worthless. They will use phrases such as "needy," "losers" and many more. The aim is to make you feel like the description of the phrase.

Chapter 7 - Abuse by a Narcissistic Mother

When Should You Talk of Abuse?

By now, you understand that narcissistic parents are abusive to their children. However, for the child of a narcissistic parent, it may be difficult to recognize that their parents are narcissists and some of them only do when they go to seek professional help for the struggles they are going through.

Narcissists come in all varieties, and the symptoms and these narcissistic tendencies vary over a wide spectrum. So how do you tell if a parent if narcissistic and abusive? Below we highlight when the maltreatment becomes abusive.

When You Become a Doormat

A narcissistic mother will often trample upon her children like a doormat, and this means that only their needs will get addressed over the needs of the rest of the family. As such, you will always find yourself bending over backward so that nobody can think you are wrong in any situation. In other instances, you find that a child has grown up being sent the message that their needs do not matter and therefore, they will let people walk all over them without knowing when to call someone out on their actions. When you find that you can no longer recognize what you need and even when you know it you cannot find the right way to express yourself then the narcissistic abuse as finally gotten to you.

A person such as this may think that voicing their own needs may result in the other person feeling that they are narcissistic because they have experienced their own narcissistic parents demanding things. A narcissistic mother is likely to make their child feel crazy or even selfish for asking for what may be considered the most basic of needs.

When You Are Afraid That You May Be a Narcissist Yourself

Sometimes, a child may not overcorrect when faced with narcissism. Sometimes, they may resent their mother's abuse so much that they do not wish to be like their mothers. However, over time, they begin to see the world in a different way. As a result, they cope by putting others down first instead of waiting for someone to put them down. If you happen to start believing that you should put people down first before they put you down first as a result of how your mother treated you, then it is likely that you have started developing narcissistic tendencies as a result of the treatment.

Children who are more likely to become narcissists as a result of narcissistic abuse are those born strong-willed and extroverted. This is generally because they possess the attitude of joining them when they can do nothing about a situation. If, therefore, you find yourself hurling insults at people and calling them names, it is likely that you are facing narcissistic abuse and you may be developing narcissistic tendencies as a result of narcissistic abuse by your mother. You will need to adjust and learn how to express vulnerabilities in terms of emotions such as loneliness, sadness, fear and when you are overwhelmed.

When You Feel That Your Siblings Are Competitors or You Resent Them

As a narcissistic mother, your parents likely view you as an extension of themselves. This causes her to develop issues with personal boundaries. If you have siblings and you were born into the home of a narcissistic parent, then this parent may choose one of you to reflect her best qualities, and thus, there may be feelings of love for this sibling at the expense of the rest of you.

For instance, they may get more praise, support, and even attention from the parents as you get nothing. Another child may be chosen to be what can be considered the scapegoat. As such, this child will be the object of shame and blame. The child will be burdened with never being right compared to the chosen favorite, and in the worst cases, they are sometimes chosen to be the children that get blamed for the parent's narcissistic behavior. These two projections represent the two sides of the personality of a narcissist. However, the effect usually is long-term, and it is not uncommon to find these siblings being rivals into their adult years and resenting each other.

The comparisons do not usually end between the two children as it is common to find these mothers comparing their children to those from other families but in the same age group. Being overly compared to peers can have a detrimental effect on the child, but a narcissistic mother often cannot realize this.

Your Mother Competes with You and Even Disrupts the Most Important Stages of Your Life

Narcissistic mothers are likely to compete with their children, especially daughters. She is likely to value her looks and sexuality over that other own daughter. Unfortunately, when a female is narcissistic, they are more likely to harbor misogynistic views and to see other women, even when they are not a threat as competition. She is, therefore, more likely to be furious, jealous and in some cases even envious of her daughter.

The abuse comes in when the woman begins to devalue the appearance of her female child. Also, part of the abuse involves body shaming and criticizing the girl as often; they feel that a person, especially their child should possess physical perfection. The damage may be extensive especially in cases where the mother will choose to cross sexual boundaries with her children, especially daughters.

A mother such as this may achieve her hideous goals by flaunting their own bodies to their children, especially girls and having inappropriate discussions about sex. Special emphasis on physical appearances is noted. Further, she may teach her children, both male, and female that they derive value from the body. The male may begin to understand that a woman must please him physically and the daughters may understand that their value is based on their body and how much they can please men.

The nature of this type of abuse can be so complicated as some of the mothers go as far as seducing the friends of their children to prove that they are sexually better than their daughters. When the culture encourages sexual restriction, the narcissistic mother may behave a little differently such that they do everything possible to stifle her daughter's newfound sexuality. The girl may, therefore, be punished for being sexually active. With such instability, it is highly possible that the narcissistic mother will fail to provide her daughters with the appropriate sexual education.

They Care About Appearances at the Expense of Everything Else

A narcissistic mother is also unlike other mothers because she creates a false illusion of being a loving, caring and even sweet mother when in reality, they only enjoy the social status of motherhood without engaging in any of the work that involves raising children.

If your mother is keen and intent on showing you out to her friends when you feel your needs such as psychological and emotional needs have not been met, then your mother is likely an abusive narcissistic mother.

She is more concerned about outside appearances rather than how things really look from within. She is also likely to ask others to help her care for her children rather than do it herself, and she will not give the care and attention that all children deserve.

Unfortunately, these mothers are more likely to treat their children as nuisances rather than ordinary people and maybe cold and even callous such that they deny the child or children the comfort of touch altogether.

She Breaks Boundaries

Narcissistic mothers are likely to be overbearing. However, this trait becomes a problem when the narcissistic mother involves herself and her children in covert emotional incest. If you are wondering what this means, it simply refers to such a mother making her children the center of her world and thus, she makes them responsible for her fulfillment emotionally.

When you look at such a case critically, you will notice that instead of fulfilling parental duties, narcissistic mothers task their children with being their parents. The children then feel like they have a sense of obligation that would require them to take care of the desires and expectations of their parents.

These mothers violate the right to privacy and even the autonomy of their children, and they may engage in behaviors that show disrespect. Some of these include demanding to know details of life that the children consider private and entering their rooms without knocking. She may also insist on reading their diaries and do thorough interrogations on their children's sexual partners and sometimes even friends.

If you analyze the activities outlined above, you will likely notice that they are designed to impede growth. As such, a child with a narcissistic mother is likely to remain in a state of perpetual childhood, and they may have problems growing up and getting out of the house in any case. They are also likely to turn down dates and have problems as they begin to explore their sexuality. Any action aimed at growing up is punished, crippling the child.

She Feels Enraged When Something Threatens Her Superiority

Narcissistic mothers, like every other narcissist, have a perceived sense of superiority. However, they do not like anything that threatens this superiority and are enraged when they meet resistance in their bid to make way for themselves to get what they want.

If you are around a narcissistic mother, therefore, you are likely to experience an emotional roller-coaster in response to her own feelings that keep on changing from time to time. When she needs something from you as her child, she is likely to love-bomb you and anytime you do not follow her rules, or you do not give in to her demands, then she is likely to get angry. There is, therefore, minimal consistency in emotions in a household with a narcissistic mother.

In such a scenario, it is not just a lack of emotional stability that is evident. The children in the house will always feel like there is a danger that stays within the confines of the house. They will walk on eggshells as a result of the fear they will have when they feel like they have offended their mother.

She Gaslights, Invalidates and Guilt-Trips Her Children

It is not uncommon for children of narcissistic mothers to react to what is obviously abusive behavior. When, however, the children react, they are not met with an apology or anything that would show that the mother feels guilty of her actions. She will shame her children for speaking up, gaslight them then invalidate their feelings and ideas to continue having that kind of control over the child. This maltreatment of her own children can be expressed as a result of the lack of empathy that most narcissists lack.

Without this sense of empathy, the narcissist cannot feel anything for her children and may even ignore their basic needs. Even after doing wrong to her children through the ways mentioned above, she will deny any form of abuse. As such, it is common to find this type of parent referring to her children as being overly sensitive and overreacting to her acts of psychological abuse.

In other cases, the mother may try to use her emotional outbursts to her own benefit and will use them to control and manipulate the children. Surprisingly, the emotions of the children will never be as important as hers as they will always be invalidated.

She, however, has the energy to guilt-trip her children to achieve her needs every time she senses that they are about to disobey her. She is also pleased when after provoking her children, she remains in power as her children suffer the guilt emotions.

By now, you should have realized that narcissistic mothers are not like every other mother who is empathetic and cares for their children's needs. Their views of motherhood are skewed, and they do not enjoy motherhood the same way normal women do.

Phases of Abuse

The phases of abuse that you will be exposed to by the narcissist are always a form of conquering that they are seeking to establish. For them to subdue you completely, they will have to idealize, devalue then discard you in that order. Below, we explore more on these concepts below:

Idealization

Narcissists are extremely calculative, and this can be seen in their ability to choose the perfect victim for their antics. Their criteria for which a child to bully and subdue comes from a variety of issues, but they are more likely to choose the child depending on what they perceive that the child can tolerate. However, in the case where a mother or a parent is narcissistic, the child usually has little or nothing to do with these qualities.

They may simply pinpoint a child who will be the victim of their abuse for the rest of their lives and pit this child against another favorite. However, the intention is the same even with the child. They have to conquer the child and continuously destroy the child.

When they realize that the child holds value, in this case, it means that the child can supply them with their needs, then they start to do what they need to do to gain their trust, and the rollercoaster begins.

Devaluation

This is a stage that is dangerous, and when referring to romantic relationships, the victim is unlikely to realize that they have transitioned from an initial stage of idealization. This is because the first stage involves love-bombing and attention and even being given compliments. However, the person who is being abused will feel that something is wrong as part of their gut feeling and not necessarily because they have experienced something out of the ordinary yet.

With children, the case is likely to be a little different. When a child has a narcissistic mother, and she/he is the only child, the parent will have a hold on them from a very early stage. It is even worse when the child has siblings, and they happen to be the ones who face the abuse rather than the favorite.

Their mothers, whether a single child or that with siblings will play the home and away game that we outlined above ad a young child may be unable to understand what is going on. This stage may be so complicated that even a grown-up victim of narcissism may not be able to figure it out.

When the child or the victim in the relationship tries to point out such shortcomings, then they will always be labeled as the crazy one or the narcissist will make them doubt their own selves. In this way, the target is confused, and then they gain the upper hand that enables them to stay in control.

Discard

The discard stage is what usually comes to a shock to many, especially those in romantic relationships. Many who have been in romantic relationships with narcissists will say that the discard is usually unexpected as it comes out of nowhere.

Usually, it comes in the form of a text message or a phone call that is meant to make them understand that they are being dismissed by the narcissist. This is usually hurtful and even cold. They will make it look like the victim has problems and that it is because of the victim that they behaved cold and hurtful. Also, they will involve themselves in something called a smear campaign where they will use the strengths of the victim as weaknesses.

Their main intention with this tactic often is to ruin the victim and make them feel worthless. When this happens, the victim's world should shut down and then they will be in a cocoon where they cannot figure out that it was the abuser and not them who had an issue.

Sometimes, the abuse at this stage has been so great that the victim is left dealing with post-traumatic stress disorder, and they are left to piece up their lives back together.

For children, the case becomes a little more complicated when their mothers are narcissistic. A parent-child relationship is more complicated because, for the rest of his/her life, a child is likely to continue interacting with their parent even in their adulthood. Some children, however, leave their narcissistic mothers in the past and do not maintain a relationship with them once they can afford to live independently.

From the stages outlined above, it is evident that being in a relationship of any form with a narcissist will drain the energy out of an individual. The children learn that the best thing to do is always to suppress their feelings. This is the reason why you find that the children of narcissists are likely to end up abusing drugs, struggling with self-harm, and they have eating disorders as well. Their lifestyles are mostly compulsive and impulsive. Luckily, it is possible to cope and even get out of a relationship with a narcissist whose only desire is to sap the energy out of you.

Types of Abuse

There are many types of abuse because they may come in different forms. For the narcissist, the way they abuse their victims is meant to achieve their goals which involve subduing the victim and making them feel worthless. Below, we discuss the different types of abuse that you will need to know to understand the mind of a narcissist.

Verbal Abuse

Verbal abuse by a narcissist is a powerful tool that they use to their advantage. This type of abuse is one that they use to wear down their victims, and they can easily convince the victim that one thing is another. It is one of their favorite tactics in the games they play.

Verbal abuse is used to intimidate the victim and helps the narcissist establish dominance. When you are a victim of verbal abuse from a narcissist, there is a likelihood of the attack catching you off guard, and this assures them that there will be victory and there will be a large probability of the person doing what the manipulator wants.

The manipulator will have a similar pattern of verbal abuse, whether they are a romantic partner, mother, or coach. As the abuse starts out, it is usually infrequent, secret and done in low tones. The abusive words are minimal, and they usually follow with an apology that is likely to be shallow. Sooner, however, matters escalate, and the abuse becomes public and is frequent, all the blame is then shifted to the victim, and the tone escalates while the perpetrator denies using abusive words.

Volume and tone, when used properly are viable tools that can help a narcissistic mother gain dominance. They will either keep quiet, ignore, or refuse to respond to you completely or they will use rage and scream and yell in your face. Either way, these two methods are effective and are used to reiterate the message of abuse.

Besides, for a narcissistic mother, words hold meaning beyond what they mean, and as such, they threaten and swear especially when the child refuses to do their bidding. Words are tools used to instill fear, threaten, manipulate, constraint and even intimidating. This speech will also feature sarcasm, competition, demands, and arguments. A narcissistic mother will not listen and will talk over their children.

They will also withhold key information, interrogate, and bully their children. To further confuse the child, a narcissistic mother will mix a bit of the truth with lies and criticism. This tactic leaves the child feeling defeated and inferior.

A narcissistic mother will always avoid embarrassment by any means. They will go on the defensive over minor things, and they commonly divert and block comments. They like to accuse their children of making them look bad. When they see someone attacking, they will react in varied ways including becoming hostile, dismiss feelings and invalidate them as well. These are not the only tactics that they use. Another famous one is how they conveniently forget that they promised someone something.

If you are looking for a master in the game of blame, then a narcissistic mother is one of your safest bets. Anything that goes wrong is the fault of the scapegoat child according to the narcissistic mother. As the victim, the child will be accused of being too critical of the mother's reaction and being too sensitive and of being oppositional. They will typically say that they are critical for the child's own good and that they are only joking. They will also commonly say that they did not abuse the victim child. A victim of narcissistic abuse feels that they can never win. They lose their self-confidence and self-esteem and feel that they can never be right. They will always walk on eggshells and will be fearful of the kind of response they give.

What you need to realize is that you are not going crazy. Verbal abuse is real when you are living with a narcissistic mother, and it will leave you confused and stressed. A general tip that you can use in your negotiation with a narcissistic mother is to avoid agreeing with anything that they say during a confrontation. Wait for at least a day before you make a decision and talk to other people so that you can get the right advice to help you make decisions the correct way. Also, remember that it is not your duty to jump into your narcissistic mother's every trap.

Financial Abuse

To understand the mind of a narcissist, think of how a pyramid scheme sells a dream to the public while only hoping to achieve their own goals through the hard work of everybody else. In romantic relationships, the partners of these people were once financially stable, and they were preyed upon by someone who charmed them and sold them a dream that was supposed to secure them a future. While selling their dreams, the narcissist leaves out the part where they are supposed to use their victims, devalue, and even abused. They do not inform the victims that they will leave them penniless and homeless.

There are some signs that you should look into as clues that a narcissist is abusing you financially, whether a romantic partner or a parent. For instance, the narcissist will always require the victim to adhere to budgetary allocations that they cannot stick to themselves. To get ahead, a narcissist will exaggerate their money muscle. Sometimes you will feel like they are using too much, and you will be tempted to ask them to stick to a budget. If you do, then be prepared to face bitterness, anger, and hostility.

Narcissists do not like a person to question their use of money, and they feel entitled and that they cannot share it even with their families. As narcissistic parents, they will feel like their children are extensions of themselves and their money are used to benefit them alone.

If you have a narcissistic mother, then it is likely that your mother will have problems spending money on you. For instance, if you have a school project coming up and you tell your mother about it, she would hesitate to help you with funds, and yet they will have to give it. Before they give it, they will have to degrade their child by saying things like they are only wasting her money.

Also, as a child of a narcissistic mother, you will need to account for every single cent. This happens even when you need resources such as budgeting tools. Keeping track of finances in a household with a narcissistic mother will not be easy. They will document all the money you spend, but they will not be expecting you to monitor the transactions they make. As such, they will always want to be in control of your paycheck. It would also not be surprising to find out that the narcissist has given out items which are yours and of sentimental value to others and sometimes, they even sell them. There is also a chance that if you are running a family business, the narcissist will force you to work at no pay. If it is your mother who is the narcissist, she will prevent you from using any money for your needs, and you will not even be able to access your accounts online without seeking permission from them.

In the worst-case scenarios, the narcissistic mother may go as far as sabotaging your job and spending your money without your permission. They will even demand that they buy you clothes and use funds from the accounts you own without any consultation. In short, it will be an emotional rollercoaster with a narcissist in your life.

Chapter 8 - Separation and Healing

The very first thing to understand about seeking freedom from a narcissist is to cut off all ties and avoid contact with them all together. For a child with a narcissistic mother, this may be difficult due to the bond you may feel you still want or could gain with them. However, narcissists are incapable of feeling empathy which makes them unable to connect with people on a deeper level. As they feel their children are an image of themselves, they will continue to bring their child down unintentionally and intentionally throughout their lives well into adulthood.

Whether a person has a narcissistic mother or someone gets involved intimately with a narcissist or they may have a close friend who has NPD, the main reason why it is so difficult to let go is because of the emotional attachment. They struggle with the idea that they can help their narcissistic relationship; that's why they stay longer than they should. It's also because the narcissist gives them the same feeling that a drug user gets from their first 'high' of a street drug of choice.

One of the things you can do to help yourself continue with a no-contact order is through writing. To be specific, make a 'trauma' journal. Trauma journals are designed to remind you of the abuse you have experienced from the narcissist. Write down what happened, how it made you feel, what you tried to do about it, etc. Write down what you remember and right when it happens. So, maybe this is a silly question, but what exactly is the no-contact rule?

- NO meeting with the narcissist – in public, private, with friends, or any other circumstance

- NO phone calls – including calling them or answering them on a friend's phone

- NO text messages – including when they try to reach you through someone you know or ask a mutual friend how they are doing

- NO social media messaging – Facebook, Instagram, Bumble, Twitter, Snapchat, Whatsapp, etc.

- NO third-party contact – including any friends, family members, or anyone associated with the narcissist

Make it known to your mutual friends or family members that you are not having any contact with your narcissistic abuser. Create some boundaries and limits for people who continue to talk about them. One thing is certain: the no-contact rule is going to be extremely difficult and may take you to an emotional

rollercoaster for the first bit of recovery. That is especially true when the narcissist happens to be your mother. The narcissist may want to lash out at you and make you feel guilty for ending the relationship and essentially getting rid of them. In their failed attempts to reach you (hopefully), they may start trying to be nice. For example, if they have reached you or still think you are getting their messages, it may start out like, "Why are you not talking to me? I thought you loved me." When the guilting, gaslighting, manipulating, and hurtful techniques wear off, they may try saying, "I am truly sorry for everything I have done to you. I miss you, so please come home, and I will do everything to make this right."

As a refresher, let's take a closer look at how it may take place.

- They may stalk you.

- They will try to reach out to you through all forms of communication, including friends, text and calls, or social media, to get the word out, etc.

- They will try to send you emails by creating endless fake accounts.

- They may act as another person to see if you respond to them.

- They may track you down and wait for you in a parking lot so that they can talk to you.

- They may come to your house unexpectedly.

If narcissists have succeeded in any of these tactics, they will manipulate you into thinking they cared for you when you were in their lives. They will butter you up with compliments about how you look so well and how you should get together for lunch. They will reminisce on all the good days disregarding any of the bad days. If you call them out on the abusive days and explain to them what you're going through even now from that, you might see them struggling to hold in their sensitivity. They may even ignore what you stated by saying they have changed and that they have really learned their lesson or have "thought about thing" since then. Expect to hear an endless supply of broken promises behind the desperation in their voice as a means to win you back as well. Remember that journal you wrote? Do not make any sudden decisions and tell the narcissist (even if it's your mother) that you will get back to them. Once you get home, open your trauma journal. Write about this experience and then flip through the pages of your abusive history. Also, if this really did happen remember that they seeked you out because you are no longer providing them with the admiration and attention they need.

If you think the narcissist might be missing you, it isn't for the reason you may think (or hope). They say that you are missed, but the cold, hard truth is that they miss what you provided for them, such as admiration, love, appreciation, and praise they were getting from you. Now that you are gone, your attention goes with you. This is why the no-contact rule is so important. At this stage in the process, they are only trying to win you back to get that back. They may truly feel a sense of emptiness and sadness; however, if they try to win you back, it's NOT because they miss you as a person.

Separation From Your Narcissistic Mother

The question now is, "Should you cut all contact with your narcissistic mother or parent?" Everything you know, love, cherish, respect, and learned from was your mother. In this sense, you have gained an emotional attachment that goes so deep into the fact that every part of growing up or being raised in the narcissistic environment makes you who you are today. The truth is that without first recognizing the relationship for what it is, you will not diminish the pain or emptiness they left on your heart. As Dr Murray Bowen says in Family Therapy, "You will continue to remain troubled and distressed if you don't work on yourself and gain prospect to internal growth." One thing to realize about your narcissistic mother is that despite all her efforts to 'win' you back, she cannot change. If she has always been non-empathetic with no remorse or responsibility for her action, she does not and will not see the damage she has caused to you. Your mother will continue her self-centered path and never realize or accept that she needs to change, unless she seeks help for her NPD herself. Even with therapy sessions and counseling to take better steps toward being a better person, it would still take many years and hard work for her to fully realize the extent of her emotions. Does this say the same for you? Not really, especially if you realize it early and make the hard decisions to continue your road to recovery. To answer the question about whether or not you should have no contact with your narcissistic mother, it may be best for a little while so that you can find yourself, figure your true values, and regain a sense of self before contacting again. You need to take this time to heal your emotional wounds, work through your trauma, and learn to be your own individual. After all, this is what your mother robbed you of your childhood. There is no certain amount of time that this will take, but if your mother respected you, they would allow you this time to grow independently without judgment. When it comes to cutting ties with your mother or family member, there are three routes you can take.

Therapeutic Services

A vulnerable or 'beginner' narcissist may be open to family or relationship counseling, which can be very enlightening for both of you with the right therapist. However, this only works if your narcissistic mother is willing to work through her childhood trauma and actually listen to the techniques mentioned in the sessions.

Civil Connection

The most common form of separation from your mother is the civil connection. This is where the abused child (adult) understands and accepts that there will be no more emotional attachments or a type of relationship with their mother. Every interaction should be civil, polite, not in-depth, or psychologically close. For this to work, the adult of the narcissistic parent needs to continue their self-work towards success and happiness. A civil connection allows the child to experience family holidays without the attachment. It gives the mother some distance to realize that she can no longer manipulate or control her child without some clear boundaries in place.

No Contact

This is essential for when the mother is too toxic that therapy and civil connection will not work (or hasn't worked). It's needed for when the mother does not understand the terms and feelings of her child even after boundaries have been set. As challenging as this may be for the child, it's the best thing they can do to gain personal recovery and healing. No child wants to separate from their parents; however, for personal growth and individuality, some sort of separation process is needed. At first, the child may feel guilty, concerned for their mother, or deeply disturbed by their overwhelming emotions. The first part of separation from anyone that you love is challenging, but as long as you state clear intentions for this process, you will be successful.

What May Happen From Cutting Ties With Your Mother

Let's say you are confident in your decision to be civil or have absolutely no contact with your narcissistic mother. The confusion is still in place, as well as the sadness of having to separate still exists, but your first therapist appointment is just around the corner. You have come to a realization that the best solution is to cut off the toxic tie. Some things your mother may try to do to you can be overwhelming but it will help you in continuing with your decision. As long as your mother does any of the following, return to your trauma journal and write it down so that you can look back on those difficult days of silence and remind yourself why this step is the best process. It's best to be prepared for what may happen in order to protect yourself and recover from the emotional abuse they put you through. They will attempt to turn the family against you if it isn't hurtful enough to have to cut ties with your mother, in her attempt to win you back, she may try to turn the family against you. If they succeed in their efforts, you may feel even more lost than ever. To protect yourself from this, make sure you let one or all family members know why you feel the need to

"break up" with your mother. If they see your side, then they will be less inclined to leave you in the dust. Make sure you do this before cutting ties with your mother so that if it happens, they will be prepared and see that you were right.

Your guilt might take over

Having self-worth and self-respect means knowing what's good for you without allowing your emotions to bring you to dark places. Yes, you will feel some guilt, but think about the trauma you experienced through her abusive, narcissistic ways. Think about what you could achieve and how you might grow as opposed to if you hadn't taken this step. If you find yourself having the urge to reach out, consider how far you have come or how much you are going to grow. Think of everything she has robbed you of and how freedom of her will allow you your full potential to succeed in life.

Family get-together may be awkward

Everyone has that one relative who serves the 'glue' of the family.

Usually, he or she wants to keep the peace and guilts you into

being civil, nice, or even attentive to the toxic person. The 'glue'

member might say, "Please be nice and talk to them for me."

Before entering a family get-together, therefore, brace yourself for your narcissistic mothers ways. Prevent your family from taking sides or forcing you to smooth things over. Your family may not notice, but in your mother's anger, she might bad-mouth you, give you the coldshoulder, or blame you for leaving her as she was the 'best' person for you. Shrug these comments off and don't take it personally. She needs to see that you will not allow her to take any more power over you and that she doesn't faze you anymore.

They might lash out at you

In the beginning or through the recovery and healing process, your mother will lash out at you unless you have successfully cut all contact. Maybe she saw it coming, or maybe she was blind-sided. The fact is that she will try to hurt you through rumors or destructive behaviors to justify her reasons for abuse with other members in the family. Make sure that you have someone you can go to when she succeeds in hurting you deeper.

The last thing that will happen is that you will feel some freedom and sense of peace from no contact and cutting ties. This will allow you to find inner sincerity and not look back. Through the rumors, manipulation, reconciliation attempts from the family, and awkward moments, you should know that you can move forward even if you are alone. Put everything else aside and understand that growth only comes from making the choice to change. Accepting and understanding yourself is the only way to continue healing.

How to Heal From Narcissistic Abuse

The emotional rollercoaster you will experience in the beginning of your recovery may be enough to mentally disarm you. The hard fact is that the longer you have endured a narcissist's abuse, the longer it will take for their poison to erase from your system. In order to overcome these deep rooted feelings of depression and anger or pain is to continue to work on yourself.

Emotional attachment

As a result from the narcissist's manipulative tactics and emotional reasoning, you may have lingering feelings of emotional attachment to them. These feelings can be extremely difficult to overcome and may be the number one reason why you want to reach out or go back.

Separation anxiety

We are taught that family is important, but to leave the narcissist sometimes means to leave the family, too. This is because the narcissistic family member can leave your narcissistic side creeping in. Separation anxiety may become the main part of why you will want to forgive your mother and smooth things over. After all, she is the main reason why you are who you are today. Instead of giving into the anxiety, take your experiences as an opportunity to grow.

Emptiness

After being a part of your mother for so long and representing her image for so long, you may not know what to do next because of her strong grasp in your life. A deep feeling of emptiness may take over as a way for you to understand the feeling of them being gone. For this reason alone, you may feel that you need their guidance and fake love to feel normal again because that is what has been normal for so long.

Independency

Throughout your life, your mother has taken your free will, state of mind, beliefs, and creative values away. You were never able to grow into yourself because your mother convinced you that you didn't have an identity. This stemmed from her jealousy and image of you. You owe it to yourself and your future healthy relationships and children to rediscover who you truly are. You can finally figure out what you like to do, what your strengths and weaknesses are, and what values you hold dear to yourself. Through this stage in the healing process, you may have to face the trauma and overcome the false reality you were raised in.

Seeking vengeance

Once you have seeked your freedom or are already in the healing stages, you may want to get back at your narcissistic abuser. You want them to feel as if you ruined their life like they did yours However, doing so will only give them power and control back because it will give them the knowledge that you still think about them. In this case, they win. Also, narcissists do not feel empathy and the best way to really get back at them is to strive for personal growth and become successful in all your wishes.

Curiosity

At times when you feel accomplished or really depressed, you may feel curious as to how they are doing or what they are doing. Say, you hadn't heard from them in a long while. Your curiosity may get the best of you which will enable you to reach out to them. If you do this, you give them power once again which allows them to intertwine their manipulative and brainwashing methods back into your life. At that point, all your personal growth and success is wasted.

Second-guessing yourself

After sometime with no communication, you may start to question yourself as to why you didn't leave sooner. Alternatively, you may second-guess your decision to leave them in the first place. You see, our minds like to ignore the negative experiences from an abusive relationship and bring forth the positive good times. When this happens, refer back to your journal so that you can recall past experiences and remind yourself why you made the right choice. Through the process of emotions you will experience, learn to be in the moment with each one. When you take your time with your internal feelings, you will get closer to healing and striving for success. Here are some ways on how you can recover through emotional healing after narcissistic abuse.

1. Learn meditation

Meditation helps in the moment, before you sleep, when you awake, and in every aspect of your life. Meditation can awaken spiritual healing and develop a deeper sense of awareness. When you are overwhelmed, take a mindful moment. When you are feeling stressed out or empty, be grateful about something. When you are restless and don't know what to do with yourself, practice yoga. Through every hard moment of your recovery process, you must meditate.

2. Grieve, be angry, be upset, and process your emotions

Many people are guilty for feeling upset, angry, confused, or emotionally distressed. This feeling only stems from the power and control the narcissist took from you. Allow them to surface and work through each one intently. As you work through them and give each emotion some attention, you will start to develop mindfulness of what triggers your emotions and be able to feel empathetic for others. It's a new sense of self-worth.

3. Follow the no-contact rule

No contact means no contact. When you feel like reaching out due to the strong emotions above, don't. Instead, call a friend or your therapist. Allow yourself to be completely in the moment with your conversation. Use distractions like watching TV or reading self-help books. Take up a new hobby or dive into work. Get your mind off the urge to reach out because there will always be a time and place for that.

4. Do not continue to obsess over narcissism Researching about narcissism is good, but constantly reading about it, trying to pick out the warning signs, and seeing it everywhere is going to make you feel insane. All you need to know are the traits and characteristics, the abuse

following NPD, and how to overcome the abuse. Once you gain this knowledge, move on to more important things in your life.

5. Build your self-esteem

The narcissistic mother has won your whole life by making you feel invalidated, insecure, invisible, and incompetent. The more self-esteem you have lost through this process, the more hold they have over you because you continuously turn to them to prove your worth and become perfect in their eyes. The hard truth is that you will never become perfect in their eyes as they always expect more. You will wear yourself down in emotional exhaustion and even that you aren't allowed to have. Remember this when you look back on your trauma. Building self-esteem is about learning how to be confident in your decisions and trusting yourself while enduring positive and healthy relationships.

If you want to completely heal, it means to look deep within yourself and find the parts of you that is missing and bring them back. For example, you don't feel confident or you feel that emotions are not necessary. True healing means rewiring your brain to be able to experience emotions again and develop confidence within yourself. If your inner critic is the thing you need to focus on, then tackle and challenge your thoughts. Create a positive mantra so that you wake up every morning without the narcissist hindering your personal growth. Understand that healing takes time and that the process of grieving comes in many forms and in many ways. You must recognize that every stage is needed for personal development, and rushing through any stage will only result in moving backwards, not forward.

Everything takes time, so give yourself time to accomplish what needs to be done for yourself and no one else.

Chapter 9 - Overcoming Enmeshment

While the codependent relationship between a mother and daughter can have many negative impacts on the daughter's life, few are as devastating as that of enmeshment. Enmeshment is the condition in which the lives of the mother and daughter are seemingly inseparable, as though they are woven together like wicker in a basket. Each life is wrapped around the other, creating the appearance of a single entity. The result is that the daughter never enjoys the life of independence and self-direction she deserves. Instead, she lives a life of utter and complete devotion to her mother, being responsible for providing happiness and wellbeing to her mother in everything she does. In the end, most enmeshed daughters become so entangled with their mother that they are no longer able to separate their own desires, thoughts, and dreams from those of their mother. They take on a mindset that is virtually hive-like in nature

In order to be free of the imprisoning consequences of enmeshment, a daughter must first recognize the symptoms of the condition and then begin taking steps to put an end to the behaviors that serve to starve them of the freedom they yearn for. This chapter will discuss some of the most common forms of enmeshment, as well as the negative influences they can have on a daughter's life. This will help anyone to determine whether or not they are the victim of enmeshment. Furthermore, this chapter will provide numerous techniques that will help the individual to begin untangling their life from that of their mother, thereby giving them the chance to achieve the independence they need in order to live a life that fulfills their full potential.

Recognize you aren't responsible for other peoples' happiness

The main type of enmeshment is that which involves the emotional wellbeing of the mother. In this case, a mother will rely on the words, actions, and emotional support of her daughter for her day-to-day happiness. A good example of this is when a mother relies on the time she spends with her daughter for the happiness and meaning she needs in her life. While such time spent together should contribute to the happiness and meaning a mother feels, what makes this scenario different is that the mother relies solely upon her daughter for this result. The bottom line is that any person should have numerous avenues through which they can find happiness, meaning, and fulfillment in their lives. Any time they rely too heavily on one or two avenues, it creates a situation of dependence. When that dependence affects another person, it creates a codependent relationship. This is why enmeshment is so devastating, as it makes the daughter feel completely responsible for ensuring that their mother is happy and content in this life.

One of the main impacts this type of enmeshment has on a daughter is that of stress and anxiety. When the daughter feels as though she alone is responsible for her mother's happiness, she will spend all of her time and energy, trying to find ways to please her mother. Sometimes the daughter might be successful, finding numerous opportunities to bring happiness and pleasure to the mother, while also having ample time to devote to this endeavor. Unfortunately, most daughters have other responsibilities, especially older daughters who have started a family of their own. Trying to juggle the needs of their own family with the emotional needs of their mother can prove more than they can handle, causing untold amounts of stress and anxiety as a result. Unfortunately, more often than not, they will sacrifice their own happiness, as well as the happiness of their family, in order to ensure that their mother is taken care of. This creates a situation where other people start to become negatively impacted by enmeshment, revealing its true destructive nature.

In order to put an end to this type of situation, it is critical for any daughter, young or old, to understand one simple principle; you aren't responsible for other people's happiness. The bottom line is that every person in life is responsible for their own happiness. A good way to illustrate this is to think of happiness like food. When a person is hungry, the only way they can satiate their hunger is to eat. Another person can bring them food, stacking plate upon the plate in front of them in an attempt to provide them with anything and everything they could possibly need. However, in the end, it is up to the individual to actually eat the food. No one can eat it for them. Happiness is much the same way. You can provide another person with all the opportunities to find happiness, but in the end, it is up to that person to partake of those things and find happiness for themselves. Furthermore, you shouldn't be the only one responsible for providing those opportunities. Instead, each person should find their own path when it comes to creating happiness for themselves.

Once you realize this truth, the next step is to begin changing your behaviors in order to put an end to the influence of enmeshment on your life. The first and most important step is to budget the amount of time and energy you spend trying to provide for your mother's emotional wellbeing. Needless to say, the opposite of being enmeshed doesn't have to be neglect. Instead, you can still spend time and energy trying to find things to do for or with your mother that will bring happiness and meaning to her life. However, you should also make sure that you spend the time you need to take care of yourself and any other people in your life, including other family members, friends, and the like. Once you restrict the time and energy you spend on your mother's emotional wellbeing; you will free yourself of the burden of being her sole caretaker in this regard. This will give you the freedom and independence you need to begin living your life, thereby creating the happiness and meaning you deserve.

Recognize you aren't responsible for other peoples' unhappiness

Just as no person is responsible for someone else's happiness, so too, no person is ever responsible for someone else's unhappiness. This holds equally true within the mother/daughter relationship paradigm. Unfortunately, mothers who practice enmeshment behavior will hold their daughters completely responsible for their misery or suffering. This is often a consequence of an unexpected pregnancy or a failed marriage that has only stayed together for the sake of the children involved. In such events, a mother can become resentful to her children, blaming them for the misery she endures each and every day in her unhappy life. Sometimes the mother is conscious of this behavior, making her actions that much more deplorable, however, more often than not this behavior is unconscious in nature, meaning that the mother is unaware of the guilt and shame she inflicts on her daughter. In either case, it is critical that the daughter recognize the dangers of this type of behavior and begins taking measures to protect themselves accordingly.

The main danger that this type of behavior poses is an overwhelming sense of guilt for the daughter. When a normal, healthy and loving person feels responsible for causing pain and suffering in someone else's life, they will become deeply affected, feeling guilt and shame for their role in the other person's misery. This guilt and shame will usually lead to an insatiable desire to make amends in any way possible. As a result, an enmeshed daughter will strive to do whatever her mother demands, hoping that in time, such servitude will compensate for any harm she has caused her mother. Unfortunately, such an outcome is never likely. Instead, the result is a state of codependency where the mother endlessly blames the daughter for her lot in life and the daughter spends her life doing anything and everything she can to try and win her mother's approval.

Putting an end to this type of codependent behavior can be a little more complicated for many daughters, especially those who legitimately love their mother and want to see them happy. The reason for this is that in this instance, the solution is more than a matter of budgeting time. In order to bring this type of behavior to an end, it is necessary for a daughter to change her mindset. This starts by recognizing the fact that you aren't responsible for other people's sadness or misery. However, that is only the beginning. Next, you have to recognize that you didn't choose to be born. Therefore, it is totally unnatural to feel guilty for your existence. It's one thing to feel guilty for something you are in control of, such as breaking a vase or saying something hateful in nature. However, coming into existence isn't one of those things. Therefore, never allow yourself to take responsibility for your birth or your existence.

The next step is to realize that your existence is actually a wonderful thing. Life is a gift, the most precious of all gifts, in fact. Your life is no exception. Therefore, any time you start to feel as though your life is responsible for the pain and suffering that defines your mother's life take the time to recognize how special and amazing you actually are. The best way to do that is to find another life, one that is also precious and amazing. If you have a pet cat, for example, spend time with your cat, giving it all the love and attention it can handle. Notice how special and amazing your cat is, and how wonderful it is to have that cat in your life. Then, recognize that how you feel about your cat is how your mother should be feeling about you. The fact that she doesn't appreciate such a wonderful gift in her life demonstrates that she is incapable of finding happiness. Thus, she is responsible for her misery, not you, nor anyone else. When you realize this truth, you will be free of the influences of enmeshment in this area once and for all.

Begin to make decisions for yourself

Perhaps the biggest step toward freedom any daughter can make is that of beginning to make decisions for themselves. After all, one of the main consequences of enmeshment is the lack of independent thought on the part of the daughter. When a person spends years of their life trying to bring happiness to someone else, the result is that they begin to mistake the other person's happiness for their own. Subsequently, they begin to identify the choices and preferences of another person as their own choices and preferences. In the end, their life turns out to be little more than an extension of the other person's life, making them a mere shadow of someone else. Unfortunately, this happens to countless numbers of daughters who are the victim of an enmeshed relationship with their mother.

In order to break free of enmeshment, it is vital that you begin to make decisions for yourself. This process will take some time and effort to achieve, as your decision-making paradigm is so ingrained in your mind that it will be difficult to start thinking about your choices from a different perspective. The first step toward making decisions for yourself is to differentiate between your own happiness and the happiness of your mother. The simple truth is that you and your mother are two different people; therefore, your hopes, dreams, and desires will be different in nature. Subsequently, in order to begin making choices for yourself, you must start by knowing what it is that will bring you true happiness. Rather than considering the choices that will make others happy, you need to focus on those things that will make you happy. These choices can be as simple as what to make for dinner, or they can be as significant as where to go to college, or what career path to follow. In the end, every single choice you have made in the past has been made in the hopes of bringing meaning, happiness, and fulfillment to the lives of others. Now it's time to start bringing meaning, happiness, and fulfillment to yourself. Needless to say, such a change in perspective, especially one that sees you putting yourself first when it comes to making choices in your life, will meet with a fair amount of backlash. Most enmeshed mothers will see such independence as a sign of defiance, born of some secret resentment or hostility toward them. Despite the fact that nothing could be further from the truth, this is the narrative that will play through the mind of most codependent mothers. Unfortunately, this is where most daughters lose their way along the journey to independence. Unable to cope with such accusations and guilt trips, they abandon their cause, return to the old ways, and begin making choices that they know will bring their mother happiness. However, the only way you will ever achieve independence, and the happy, fulfilling life such independence can bring, is to stand your ground, even in the face of harsh, resentful opposition. This won't be an easy transition, but it is one that is necessary in order to make positive improvements to your life. Thus, it is imperative that you begin assessing each and every decision you make in terms of what will bring you the most happiness. Only then can you start living your life, rather than letting someone else live it for you.

Become self-aware

An important element of making a choice yourself is knowing what it is that will actually make you happy. Most victims of codependent relationships struggle with the notion of self-identity, having spent their lives living someone else's life instead of their own. The biggest problem is that the freedom a person gains from their codependent past is of no value if that person doesn't know what to do with their life once they are in control of it. Therefore, it is absolutely essential that you take the time and effort needed in order to become self-aware. In short, this is the process that will enable you to know what you think, how you feel, and more importantly, what you want when it comes to making any and every decision that presents itself in your life. Only then can you know that the life you are living is truly yours and yours alone.

The first step toward becoming self-aware is to analyze your thoughts and feelings. Only by examining the contents of your heart and mind can you begin to determine what belongs there and what needs to be purged. A good way of achieving this goal is to keep a journal. You can use your journal to make lists, thereby taking the contents of your heart and mind and putting them on paper for your eyes to see. Once you see these lists, you will be able to recognize those things that belong to you as opposed to those things that belong to others. Whenever you see ideas, thoughts, or desires that aren't truly yours, you can cross them off your list, leaving only the items that belong to you. Eventually, you will be left with a list of things that will bring your life the meaning and happiness you deserve, and this will serve as the roadmap for you to follow in order to fulfill your dreams.

The second step toward becoming self-aware is to analyze the consequences of the choices you make. Do your decisions bring you pleasure? Do they serve to create the life you desire and deserve? If so, then they are the decision you should make each and every day. However, if they fail to achieve that goal, then you need to take the time to reconsider your decisions making process. This is another situation where a journal can prove invaluable. By recording specific choices and decisions you make, along with the consequences that they bring, you can track the progress of your life. As long as your choices take you in the direction you want to go, they are the right ones. However, any time they fail to bring you the happiness and purpose you desire, it is time to make changes. Sometimes the decisions that fall short are vestiges of the past, echoes of the desires and dreams others planted in your mind. Once you recognize this, you can eliminate those from your mind, replacing them with your own dreams and desires. This will help you to break free from the emotional and mental control that others have exercised over you for your entire life.

Accept the truth

Finally, there is one simple truth that must be accepted before a person can truly move past enmeshment and all of the power it wields. That truth is that you cannot fix your mother. Although the happy ending in made-for-TV movies would have you believe that as you fix your life, you will somehow also fix your mother's life as well, this simply isn't the case. If you were able to fix how your mother lived her life, you would have done so long ago. The fact that you haven't demonstrates that it is beyond your abilities. Knowing this is a critical part of the process that will allow you to leave the past behind and start living the life you deserve.

This doesn't mean that you can't still feel sympathy and compassion for your mother. In fact, it means quite the opposite. When you accept that you can't fix your mother's life, you can begin to feel compassion for her in a way that is healthy and safe. Instead of allowing that compassion to affect your decision-making process, now you can live your life freely while also showing concern for your mother and her life-condition. The bottom line, however, is that this process is about you fixing your life, and that is where your focus and efforts should be. By fixing your life you can't make up for the pain and suffering that has defined your mother's life, but you can ensure that her pain and suffering won't affect anyone else ever again, including your family and, more importantly, yourself.

Conclusion

I truly hope that this book has been able to shed some light on what it is to deal with a narcissistic mother and how to handle it as an adult. The time you have taken and invested in this book is greatly appreciated. While a lot of information was covered, there is plenty more to be learned about narcissism and how it affects us, overall.

The effects that narcissism can have on a daughter is astounding but, with hard work and dedication, the negative impact can absolutely be corrected. Learning to understand who you are dealing with and the effects your narcissistic mother has had on you are only the first steps in becoming mentally and emotionally balanced.

Becoming emotionally intelligent and learning the true intentions of those around us can also aide in ensuring we pursue healthy, rather than toxic, relationships. It can also open our eyes to the toxicity that some people bring to the table. If you can see these things as they are coming, you can avoid being taken advantage of.

Alongside emotional intelligence comes social skills and empathy. These are both key elements in finding true happiness and balance in one's life. We can accomplish these things by practicing the art of neuro-linguistic programming as well as practicing exercises associated with Cognitive Behavioral Therapy.

Keeping yourself protected from emotional and mental abuse is something we all need to learn. It leads to a more productive life with healthier relationships. Having an understanding of toxic people and how they work will allow us to gain insight into how to deal with them. This can enable us to build strong relationships with everyone we come into contact with.

Printed in Poland
by Amazon Fulfillment
Poland Sp. z o.o., Wrocław